MUSSOLINI:
The Tragic Women in His Life

Translated from the Italian
and with an Introduction by
Graham Snell

MUSSOLINI:
The Tragic Women in His Life

by Vittorio Mussolini

THE DIAL PRESS
New York, 1973

Italian edition first published in Italy under the title *Due Donne nella Tempesta*

Library of Congress Cataloging in Publication Data
Mussolini, Vittorio, 1916–
Mussolini: the tragic women in his life
1. Mussolini, Benito, 1883–1945. I. Title
DG575.M8A353   945.091′092′2 [B]   73–3453

Introduction

There is a vast array of books on every aspect of Fascism, and several scholarly studies of its founder, Benito Mussolini. Of those written by English historians the most celebrated—and justly—is F. W. Deakin's *The Brutal Friendship*. And inevitably there are glimpses of the dictator in the memoirs, letters and historical studies of a host of wartime leaders, Churchill and Lord Avon among them. But still relatively little is known about Mussolini the family man . . . or about the Mussolini women.

Nobody could be better qualified to fill this gap than the dictator's eldest son, Vittorio. He was, though a very young man at the time, entrusted by his father with important missions. And he was (and still is) close, with an Italian family closeness, to his mother and his brothers and sisters.

One of his father's greatest gifts was with words. A commanding orator and a lifelong journalist, Mussolini was editor of the Socialist weekly *La lotta di classe* and, later, of *Avanti*, the newspaper of the Italian Socialist Party; he also founded another weekly, *Il Popolo d'Italia*, which was to become the official organ of Fascism; for years, too, he was a contributor to the American press. So well did the Duce love to exercise this gift, that at the height of the war he found time to write a book dedicated to his middle son Bruno, killed in an airplane accident, as well as innumerable articles and letters.

In one sense Vittorio is very much his father's son, for he too is a journalist and author. In this the first of his books to be translated into English, he focuses on the three women his father really loved—Donna Rachele, Countess Edda Ciano and Clara Petacci; the Duce's wife, daughter and mistress respectively. To all of them came misfortune or worse.

To the beautiful Clara, who chose to stay with her lover to the end when she could have accompanied her parents to safety in Spain, came violent death: she and Mussolini were machine-gunned at point-blank range by partisans on a narrow mountain road near Lake Como; their bodies were taken to Milan and hung head-down from a girder at a filling station in the Piazzale Loreto.

To Donna Rachele, loyal wife, came widowhood and a spell of imprisonment.

And to the impetuous Edda, wife of Count Ciano (Italy's Foreign Minister and, later, Ambassador to the Vatican) came a double loss. For she too was widowed, but the circumstances of her husband's death—he was shot in the back by a firing squad while seated with his hands tied round the back of a chair—drove her, at least temporarily, to hate her dictator father, as she was convinced he could have saved the Count.

Galeazzo Ciano was one of nineteen men who, in the Fascist Grand Council, in the early hours of July 25, 1943, voted for the famous Grandi motion. Dino Grandi, who before the war was Italian Ambassador in London, had proposed in his motion that, since the dictatorship had led the Italian people and nation to disaster and since defeat at the hands of the Allies was certain, the Duce should give up his dictatorial powers and the King (Victor Emmanuel III) should take command of the armed forces. In the afternoon of July 25, Mussolini had an audience with the King, who insisted on the Duce's resignation. When Mussolini emerged from the Villa Savoia, he was arrested by *Carabinieri* officers. Marshal Badoglio was made Head of Government.

Mussolini was imprisoned—first on the island of Ponza, then on the more secluded island of La Maddalena, off Sardinia. He was later moved, for fear of German rescue attempts, to a mountain-top hotel in the Apennines. But Hitler had detailed Otto Skorzeny, commander of a special SS Commando unit, to free the Duce. On September 12, 1943, eight gliders and a small Storch aircraft landed on the mountainside. Mussolini, escorted by a triumphant Skorzeny, was snatched away to Germany. In the meantime—on September 8—the Badoglio Government had surrendered to the Allies and the enraged Germans had seized Rome.

Once the Germans had set Mussolini up in power

again—the seat of his new Government was Salo, on Lake Garda—hardline Fascists clamored for vengeance on the men who had voted for Grandi's motion. Of the nineteen signatories, thirteen had disappeared—Grandi himself had fled to Lisbon. So six men—one of them Count Ciano, the Duce's son-in-law—were put on trial for their lives.

Such is the background to the events Vittorio Mussolini describes in his book. He saw his father torn between political survival (which demanded Ciano's death) and the passionate, angry appeals of his spirited daughter . . . his firstborn and, many have said, his favorite child, battling for her husband's life. (Vittorio had earlier seen his sister turn her fiery temper on Hitler and Von Ribbentrop.)

If the fate of Count Ciano caused an agonizing rift in the Mussolini family, the Duce's affair with Clara Petacci was another source of distress. Vittorio saw the effect it was having on his mother, and took the courageous step of talking to his father about it. That bitter interview showed him, as he relates in his book, that Clara was not like the numerous other women the Duce had enjoyed and discarded: she was special. He is frank about his father's love life, and he reveals that his mother knew nothing of the affair with Clara until an amazingly late stage—so that the shock of discovery was all the greater.

I wanted to meet the man whose book I was translating. We had arranged to have a drink at the hotel where

I was staying in Bologna, one evening in April this year. Soon after seven o'clock the phone in my room rang. "Il Dottor Mussolini is waiting for you in the hall," the receptionist said.

I walked down: I wanted time to collect my thoughts. He was looking up the wide staircase, as if he knew I wouldn't use the lift. I moved toward the eldest son of the man who for twenty-one years was supreme ruler of Italy and the western world's first twentieth-century dictator. Vittorio Mussolini was dressed in a well-tailored gray pinstripe, and in one hand behind his back he held a soft brown trilby. With him was his handsome wife.

Ever since he left Italy at the end of 1946 he has made his living as a journalist. When his father met his grisly end, one sort of life ended for Vittorio Mussolini and another—a quiet family life mostly lived in the Argentine—began. But to be the son or daughter or wife of a revolutionary dreamer who—rare combination—has also a ruthless instinct for power, is a very special fate. To meet Vittorio Mussolini, and to read his book, is to be made aware of what such a fate can be like.

G.S.

Sunbury-on-Thames
November 1972

ix

I

The gossip columns have had their day with Mussolini, but it's still too soon to attempt a historical appraisal. Time, it's true, has already set part of the record straight, and I am sure this process will one day be complete—though perhaps we won't live to see that day. Anyway, what good would it do if I tried to force the issue by digging into other people's lives for fresh evidence?

But there is another story, a very different one, which might be worth telling: it's the story of our family, consisting, like any other, of men and women, even if our name is Mussolini—something we have never been able to forget or escape. I remember all the characters in this story, their joys and their sorrows. They were my own flesh and blood, and we shared many years together. But above all I remember my mother and my sister Edda. Often, when I sit down at the table with my wife and children, I find myself looking around for my mother and brothers and sisters as if they were only in the next room. It's then that I remember with the greatest wrench the days when we really sat round the same table, in the Villa Torlonia [the dictator's family residence in Rome], with my father, and glanced at his face to see if he was tired or worried, as all wives and families do when the head of the family comes home from work. We usually lunched at about two o'clock, in an oval room full of statues. Papa didn't eat much—a little pastasciutta, some wholemeal bread, boiled vegetables, mixed salad, fruit. In front of him there was always a big saltcellar in which he dipped celery and beans and his favorite—fennel. He didn't drink wine or coffee, and he ate with incredible speed. He took absolutely no pleasure in his meals; often he wouldn't sit down until everything had been brought in, from the first course to the fruit.

And yet there came a day when it didn't matter anymore, and for the first time I saw my father wait to be served. That day was different from any other, and I still remember it with unspeakable anguish—it was September 19, 1943, in Munich. My father had been liberated a week before, and it was the first time since July 25 [the day Mussolini was arrested, after the vote in favor of Grandi's motion of censure in the Fascist Grand Council] that we had all been together, safe and sound . . . for the time being at least. There were ten of us—my father and mother, myself, my brother Romano, my sisters Anna Maria and Edda, Galeazzo Ciano and his three children, Fabrizio, Marzio and Raimonda. We had all arrived recently in Munich. Edda and Galeazzo had been there about a month, waiting to get away to Spain; I had been there only a few days—from Konigsberg, where I had stayed since July 28, I had come straight from the Fuehrer's General Headquarters with my father. My mother, Romano, and Anna Maria had arrived from Rimini in a German airplane only the previous day.

The Germans had been very kind to us. My mother had received big bunches of flowers for our family reunion, and the Foreign Minister had placed at our disposal a whole floor of the former Karl Palace, a sumptuous old building in Munich. I can still see that vast dining room, those high windows, the chandeliers, the big Flemish pictures full of animals and flowers in warm colors against a mysterious murky background, and the carpets on which impeccable orderlies in white jackets moved noiselessly. My father sat at the head of the table, in an old carved chair. He was in a dark civilian suit, with a tie that had been hurriedly and carelessly knotted. He had his back to a window: the play of light veiled his features, and yet they were changed by fatigue and grief. He was thinner and obviously suffering, and only his eyes, deep and commanding, had conserved something of their force.

After a few minutes the orderlies served the soup—a rather watery vegetable broth. Papa took only a few spoonfuls, with no relish. I could see he was deep in thoughts far removed from us, perhaps also from himself. On his right sat my brother-in-law Galeazzo in his usual aloof manner, which so angered my mother.

He was wearing a light-gray suit, perfectly cut, and

out of his breast pocket a crisp white handkerchief protruded with casual elegance. His hair was carefully combed, his nails immaculately cut. From time to time he even managed to make us smile, commenting to me on the modest lunch, which after the soup consisted only of duck, a few boiled potatoes and a piece of horrible yellow synthetic butter. He and my father had already had a talk before we sat down at the table, and my father knew perfectly well that the vote taken by the Grand Council had shocked and outraged the Fascist masses, and even more so the Germans, and that Galeazzo's position was anything but secure. And yet my father had already forgiven him; he had much more important—though less personal—problems to resolve, and for the moment he was intent on bringing his authority to bear on Hitler so that his son-in-law might escape unscathed from the trap about to close on him. As for Galeazzo, I don't believe he appreciated the full significance or, above all, the consequences of what he had done, together with the other members of the Grand Council. He refused to believe that at that moment he was the most hated man in Italy: the Fascists blamed him, politically, for the *coup d'état* and, personally, for having brought about the fall of his father-in-law's régime; the anti-Fascists accused him of having tied Italy closer to the Germans; and the Germans held him directly responsible for Italy's political and military collapse, with all that it meant for their own country.

As we ate, senior German officers and diplomats would appear from time to time in the doorway. The officers, nearly all in the SS, were convinced that my father would not sit at the same table with his son-in-law, and I think they stuck their heads around the dining-room door in the secret hope of witnessing some violent scene. With the diplomats it was different. I've always thought diplomats are a species quite distinct from the rest of the human race. Perhaps it's the demands of their profession, perhaps it's innate in them, but they are all—no matter what country they come from—more favorably disposed to others than to their own countrymen—and they then claim special immunity. I saw an example that day. They regarded Ciano in quite a different light from that in which the German military authorities saw him. I would say they were almost pleased that one of their own number, a diplomat, had played a key part in a collapse of such proportions, irrespective of whether it had damaged the common cause; and it must also be said that in ironclad Germany itself plans were being hatched that were to lead to the attempt on the Fuehrer's life.

When I looked away from my father and brother-in-law toward my sister and mother, I received an even stronger and more painful impression. Someone has said that in life's supreme moments a man still manages to hold back something of himself, whereas a woman is solely and utterly a woman . . . and I began to be persuaded of it at that moment. Next to me Edda, silently trying to swallow a few mouthfuls, was oblivious of everything other than how to save her husband. It was her instinct, rather than specific German opposition to plans for the whole Ciano family to escape to Spain, that told her Germany was the really mortal danger for her family. Galeazzo, after the talk with my father, had tried to buck her up, saying he was convinced of his innocence and therefore confident of the understanding and protection of the Duce; but for Edda the Duce, the Fuehrer, the war, the alliance were all meaningless words. To escape—that was all that mattered, so much so that anybody who thought otherwise automatically became an enemy to her, even my father who was in fact risking what was politically his most precious asset —the loyalty of his last followers and the support of his German allies—precisely in order to save his daughter's husband. And Galeazzo had agreed to return to Italy to face whatever was coming. ("After all," he had told me, "I'm still a lieutenant colonel in the Air Force. They'll send me to the front and then they'll see if I can fight for my country and the Duce.") But if Edda distrusted Germany, she also distrusted Italy. She knew that Galeazzo could no longer count on anybody's support, not even that of Alessandro Pavolini [he became Secretary of the Fascist Republican Party and was shot at Dango by the partisans], who had been one of his most loyal friends. The Fascists who had returned to my father were insisting that the traitors of July 25 should pay dearly for what they had done. Ciano was one of them and Ciano should pay—that was what everybody thought then. Edda knew it and was ready to fight— fight anybody.

I remember that during that lunch, which was very quiet on the surface, Edda's eyes sometimes met my mother's. They would both fall silent or talk about trivial things, because in my father's presence none of us dared be contentious, although July 25 and its consequences must have come between my mother and sister. Edda was wrapped up in her problem. My mother was immersed in a different set of problems; she was goaded, moreover, by bitter thoughts, and a thousand torturing doubts assailed her, so that political matters and personal worries all merged into one nightmare.

July 25 had seen the end of a struggle to which not only my father but she, too, had given a lifetime of passion, sacrifice, hardship, fears, and hopes, and it had produced only a triumph for "the others," for those who belonged to a world that was essentially different from hers, a false conventional world where nobody ever settled a difference by shouting and coming to blows, if that's what was needed, but instead bowed and smiled so they could more easily knife one another in the back. There was one man who typified all this for my mother, and that was Badoglio [Marshal Badoglio became head of the Italian Government in Rome after July 25 and surrendered to the Allies on September 8, whereupon the Germans seized Rome]. So she hated him furiously, recognizing in him an ever-present hostility she had sensed for years, which had been forced at last to come out into the open.

But how had it come about?

It was here that my mother, temperamentally unsuited as she is to understand political subtleties, was bound to find herself on the barricades facing Galeazzo. Certainly July 25 had been brewing for a long time; it had been fashioned by a complex series of remote causes and effects, but as in all decisive events in history, a chance occurrence had set the mechanism of the plot in motion—in this case the vote in the Grand Council. And hadn't Galeazzo voted by any chance in favor of Grandi's motion?

The meager meal of roast duck and boiled potatoes was over, and my father was picking up the crumbs around his plate—a habit of his. Next to him Galeazzo lightly wiped his lips with a corner of his napkin and slowly drank a glass of Moselle wine. Edda and my mother watched them both silently.

The children, who had had to sit and keep quiet too long, began to show signs of restlessness. "They'd better go and play," my mother said. And in a flash they were all away from the table. My sister Anna Maria, who was then fourteen, took the bib off Marzio, who was running off with it still on. "What a bundle of energy that child is," commented my mother—and for a moment we all smiled again. Even my father seemed to emerge from his thoughts to watch those innocent creatures, happily unable to appreciate that it was a false security that surrounded us, one that was charged with drama.

An orderly arrived with a tray of coffee. It was typical German coffee, pale and watery. We drank it in silence while my father went on slowly picking up crumbs. Now that the children had left the table, the whole atmosphere seemed gloomier. I looked at the empty chairs, the leftovers on the plates, the uneaten bits of bread, and the empty glasses, and my heart ached. For a moment I had the odd sensation that I was dreaming. Perhaps none of this is true, I thought. Now I'm waking up and it'll all be different. But I wasn't dreaming.

A German officer came in, stooped, and in a low voice said something in my father's ear. My father stood up. Decisions had to be made whether the Duce was to return to Italy and about where the new Fascist Government was to be set up. My father wanted instinctively to go back to Rome. He didn't care that this would mean even greater danger for the already precarious new Government, since the Allies were advancing toward central Italy. The German military took a quite different view and objected, above all because Rome was an open city. But I believe that more than anything else they feared the presence of the Duce in the capital of what had once been his empire. They knew what immense powers of recovery their ally still had, and they realized these might threaten their plans to make themselves total masters of Italy and take command of every sector of our national life with no semblance of Italian authority. The German military wanted my father to remain in Germany, so that they could get their hands on Italy; and the only reason they didn't have their way was that Hitler put his foot down, though he had to agree that the new capital should not be Rome.

In the last few months resistance to Hitler had hardened and grown among the German generals, though it was impossible to tell just how far it went.

Among the thousand problems that faced my father in reconstituting the Government—problems that would undoubtedly have overwhelmed the average man—the question of Rome was the most important, but not the most trying. Much more harrowing, both because it involved his personal affections and because it touched on the most delicate aspects of his standing with the Germans and the Fascists who had returned to their posts ready to fight, was the problem of deciding Ciano's fate. Already in those first days of regained freedom, on German territory, my father had done everything humanly possible to help him. He had given the Fuehrer an undertaking that he would answer personally for his son-in-law, and he had great faith in the assurances Hitler had given him. Galeazzo, for his part, had faith in my father. But my mother was far removed from this problem. The fate of her son-in-law (and therefore the future of her daughter and grandchildren) and the bitter disappointment of Ciano's behavior—to my mother, all this counted for nothing beside matters concerning her husband, the only man who was really important to her. It was up to the rest of us, each and every one, to face the consequences of our actions.

My father left us with a tired wave. When he had gone out of the room, Edda and Galeazzo got up to go back to the villa at Almashausen where the Germans had provided them with accommodation. The children had gone to play in a big room near the dining room, where they had found a piano.

Romano, I remember, was playing a boogie-woogie— as best he could, of course, because at that time his entire musical experience had been crammed into Badoglio's forty-five days, during which he had been shut up in the castle of La Rocca delle Caminate [the

Mussolini country home near Forli, Romagna] with an old piano for his only amusement. I rushed over to stop him playing: he was very fond of jazz, just as I was, but he was too young to appreciate that political considerations, especially the fact that we were guests of the Germans, made it inadvisable to play music associated with the enemy.

He realized his mistake in a flash and, to make amends, he launched laughingly into a selection of Viennese waltzes. I came away with Edda's children. My mother kissed them one by one and said good-bye to my sister. Galeazzo moved toward the door. Then he stopped and said rather curtly, "Let's go." Edda and the children followed him out.

Shortly afterwards I heard the noise of a car roaring away.

Only my mother and I had remained in the big dining room. I shall always remember the look she had in her eyes. She was staring into space, but she wasn't crying. Mother has always been a strong person, but perhaps that day she should have cried, bitterly and openly, like any other woman, and I knew why.

On July 25 my father had fallen from his position as head of the government, victim of a plot; but at the same time he had fallen, so far as my mother was concerned, as a husband—and it had been all the more painful for her in that she had only just then found out about his affair with Clara Petacci.

I've often thought back on this particular chapter in our family's private life, and have been amazed that my mother was the last to find out about what was, by then, public knowledge, even abroad. What makes it all the more amazing is that my mother had an extraordinary ability to pick up all sorts of information (and to get it she would even go so far sometimes as to disguise herself), which she promptly passed on to my father. It might be the excesses of some Party official, or a grouse from a midwife, or whispered gossip about top military brass or grand ladies of the aristocracy. My mother took note of it all with the shrewdness and fierce watchfulness that she had developed during many years of mortal political combat at my father's side. Yet here was something that concerned her and only her, and it seemed that some mocking conspiracy of silence had put her off the scent.

To express a point of view with which probably only men will agree, I must say that my father never, in any way, allowed his love affairs, even the one with Clara Petacci, to detract from his relations with my mother or with the rest of us, and they never lessened the respect and affection that we all felt for him, even if the Petacci affair had far more serious consequences than his other adventures, especially in its tragic outcome. There were numerous love affairs in my father's life, as there are in the lives of many men . . . and I'm not going to cite examples (though if I did, it would raise a deal of scandal) from among those who later shared out the power spoils in Italy. I don't set myself up as a judge of morals—something which those others did with great zeal at the time and have continued to do ever since.

It was Edda, I remember, who first told me that my father had love affairs. I was still a small boy then, and it shook me terribly . . . and I believe it's the same for any boy when he realizes that his father, for all the fact that he's his father, can still be attractive to a woman other than his mother. Edda, like my mother, was very scornful about it. She said that my father was attracted to rather ugly women, and that by accepting their favors he showed very poor taste. At that time I didn't bother much about this aspect of the matter. The mere thought of another woman, beautiful or ugly, getting her hands on the wealth of affection that was our family's property, filled me with anger and fear and at the same time doubled my affection for my mother, whom I felt I must defend at all costs, above all by preventing her from finding out.

I had an affectionate and generous father who was also—though here again I know only men will understand me—a good husband. I myself, when I had left childhood and its confused fears behind me, and had acquired greater understanding of such human problems, never attached very great importance to these affairs, not even the one with Clara Petacci. I had known practically all about her from the outset, and my only concern had been that my mother should not have this new worry added to the many grave ones she had already. I hoped the affair would soon finish, as had happened before, but I was forced to realize as time went on that this woman's attachment to my father was really strong and that the affair was something out of the ordinary.

Events, moreover, were to bear me out. But what annoyed me most was that my father's enemies were presented with an opportunity to mount a smear campaign and thus do him fresh harm. In politics, or rather a certain type of politics, abundant use is made of such methods, and I saw the Petacci affair grow into a vast scandal with the encouragement of certain factions and holier-than-thou hypocrites.

But it was natural that my mother should take a quite different view of the affair, a view that was totally and exclusively feminine. The newspapers and the radio had already given out the news that Clara Petacci, who had been put in prison immediately after my father's arrest, had been released. This opened up the possibility, perhaps even certainty, that she and my father would meet again as soon as my father returned to Italy.

I sensed that these were my mother's thoughts in the oppressive silence of that vast dining room, and I felt for her—how could I do otherwise? On the other side of the door, in the room that served as an improvised study, the Duce and several Italian and German colleagues were studying the constitution of the new Government and the choice of a new capital. I was sure that at that moment my father was applying all his energies to these objectives, and no doubt his only concern was that nothing should be left out of account.

But my mother's mind was on something else. On the other side of the door from my father, all she could see was the other woman, the woman who at that moment was aching to see my father, to give him all her love once again.

I would have liked to go up to my mother, put my arms around her, and tell her that none of this mattered

—but it wouldn't have helped. My mother was alone with all her woman's desperation, and so she would have to remain. All I could do was stay there with her and say nothing. The orderlies were clearing the last things off the table. I watched in a daze as the white-gloved hands cleared the plates and cutlery and glasses. Then one orderly took off the tablecloth, and another replaced it with a long damask runner. He deftly spread it out, adjusting it with quick little dabs.

We were alone again, my mother and I.

Then the door of the study opened and a German officer motioned me to enter. I found my father looking very worried. "The Germans," he said as soon as they had left us alone, "are suspicious of us. Sometimes I get the impression they even suspect me, as if I engineered July 25, or at least connived at it. Anyway, it's obvious they're watching us and they expect us to take firm steps, the first of which is the trial of the Grand Council members who voted for Grandi's motion. The Fascists are worse still—they take an even harder line than the Germans. For the time being the only solution is for Galeazzo to go back to Italy."

I said, "Let's hope for the best." I had been with the Germans for about two months and I knew exactly how they saw things, just as I knew what the Fascists thought. There was nothing more to be done. Death was already hovering over our family. I said again, "Let's hope for the best." Then I bade my father good-bye. He had charged me with a personal mission. An hour later I was boarding a fighter bomber of the Luft-waffe, on my way to Rome.

II

"The *coup d'état* of July 25 confronted Italy with the greatest act of treachery in recorded history. A sinister plot involving the King and certain generals, Party leaders, and ministers who more than any others had done well out of Fascism, stabbed the regime in the back and created disorder and confusion in the country at the agonizing moment when the enemy was setting foot on the soil of the fatherland. The King's treachery can be left to the judgment of the people and of history; it is only right, however, that the treachery of those who have not only failed in their duty as citizens but also broken their oath as Fascists should be severely repressed and punished. The conscience of the betrayed Fascist masses, and the memory of our fallen martyrs, demand it. Neither can we leave unpunished the acts of violence and the outrages committed by certain persons who, taking advantage of a sudden license and the complicity of those who had seized power, attacked people and property belonging to the regime, thinking that it was dead and buried. Therefore the following decree has been issued. . . ."

I put my hand out to the little radio on the bedside table and switched to another station. I knew already what the broadcast was about. The previous day, October 27, 1943, the RSI [Italian Social Republic] had approved the setting up of tribunals in every province as well as the Special Tribunal. It was the task of these tribunals to judge the Fascists who had "in any way, in speech, writing or other means, denigrated Fascism and its institutions and committed acts of violence against the persons or property of Fascists."

The penalty for "traitors of the Idea" was to be death.

Hard words. They were to remain mere words, at least so far as they applied to the provincial tribunals, which in fact passed very few sentences, and then only light ones. But the Special Tribunal was another matter.

The hostility that the Fascist masses felt for those members of the Grand Council who had voted for Grandi's motion had become irresistible. In every reassembled branch of the Fascist Party, meetings would close with a demand for exemplary punishment.

On October 28 [anniversary of the 1922 March on Rome, following which Mussolini came to power], in an atmosphere truly reminiscent of the days of Jacobin terror, a meeting of the Bologna branch of the Fascist Republicans had passed a motion demanding that the Costituente [the Fascist Assembly] should recognize "Victor Emanuel III guilty of treason against the State, having committed acts directed at placing the territory of the State under the sovereignty of another and enemy State, and at jeopardizing its independence." The motion therefore demanded "the death penalty and the confiscation of belongings for all members of the House of Savoy, with the exception of the family of the heroic Duke of Aosta, the death penalty and confiscation of belongings for Badoglio, Ambrosio, Roatta and the other generals and admirals who showed complicity in the infamous betrayal, and the death penalty and confiscation of belongings *for each and every one* of the nineteen signatories of Grandi's motion." The allusion to Ciano, who had been arrested some days before, as soon as he got off the airplane that brought him back to Italy, was obvious. As I had feared, my brother-in-law's fate was surely pointing in one direction, and only a miracle could save him. I must say that Edda believed in that miracle up to the very last moment. She screamed, she wept, she threatened, she turned against everybody, including my father and mother. They were terrible days for all of us.

My father had returned from Germany and resumed his position as leader, first at the castle of La Rocca delle Caminate (which had been presented to my father by the Province of Forli, and was his much loved country retreat), and then at Gargnano on Lake Garda, where he had set up the Government. I had been elected Secretary of the Fascist Republican branches in Germany and I had to shuttle between Rome, Gargnano, Munich, and Berlin. It was known that Hitler and the other German leaders liked me and held me in some regard. And this factor weighed with those who elected me (it was the first election of a democratic nature I had ever taken part in). The post involved the very delicate task, among others, of looking after the Italian internees, who were growing every day more numerous and more disorganized, as well as the free workers. Edda, who had moved to Rome as soon as Galeazzo was arrested, knew of my good relations with the Germans and was counting on me for the execution of her plan. We could all guess at the ultimate objective of this plan, but as for the details which my sister had secretly worked out with her exceptional determination—these for the most part were unknown to us.

Anyway, Edda came to see me. Today, at this considerable distance of time, I realize that the quiet way she spoke on that occasion was all part of her plan—and an important part. I came to the conclusion that Edda was being cunning with me, and to a certain extent that was so. But I never held it against her. On the contrary, I admired her all the more for the brave tenacity with which she was prepared to follow her chosen path as a woman, alone and against everybody, even against those who loved her.

"I can't stand being without my children," she said. "You must go and get them for me. You're friendly with the Germans. They can't refuse you. Please, Vittorio, bring me back my children."

Edda, like my father, has always had a remarkable way of persuading people by fixing them with a stare. There's no Napoleonic bullying, just an extraordinary intensity, almost—odd as this may sound—a kind of gentleness.

"All right, I'll go. But you know what they're like. They present you with flowers, and then don't give you an inch if they don't want to."

Edda nervously stubbed out her cigarette and looked at me. "Yes—the flowers. Do you remember?"

She was referring to September 3, 1943. Edda and Galeazzo, relying on a promise made by Colonel Dollmann [Himmler's representative in Rome], had gone to Germany convinced they would be able to proceed to Spain; but from the first moment in Germany they sensed they had fallen into a trap. So Edda asked for a personal audience with Hitler. This was immediately granted, so quickly in fact that it seemed, superficially at least, that the Fuehrer's friendship for our family, and also for Edda, was the same as ever. The meeting took place in the little sitting room in Hitler's personal train, about a hundred kilometers from Konigsberg, in an enormous forest that stretches around the Masurian Lakes, almost on the frontier with Lithuania. I was there too: they had sent for me in a car just before the meeting, and the last thing I had expected was to see my sister. Edda told me about the arrangement between Galeazzo and Dollmann. Having learned a little about the mood of the Germans, I was worried and didn't hide this from Edda, as I was sure that she and Galeazzo had really placed themselves in the lion's mouth. But we weren't able to discuss it any further because an officer ushered us into the presence of the Fuehrer and Von Ribbentrop.

As soon as we entered the sitting room my sister was presented with two magnificent bunches of flowers, with good wishes for her birthday. I had forgotten all about the birthday, and so had Edda herself. But not the Germans—whose attention to ceremony was impeccable, even at the most difficult moments. We sat down on a comfortable dark leather sofa. The flowers had cheered us up: they seemed a good omen. But we were soon to think otherwise. When Edda began to hint at her wish to leave for Spain with Galeazzo and the children, and mentioned that she was somewhat surprised that Dollmann's promise had still not been kept, the faces of Hitler and Von Ribbentrop swiftly changed.

"Count Ciano is being well looked after," said Von Ribbentrop, "in keeping with his rank." Perhaps there was something not quite as it should be? Von Ribbentrop was very courteous and seemed ready to sack all the servants at the Almashausen villa where Edda and Galeazzo were staying—and it was all too clear that he was deliberately trying to provoke my sister, knowing it would be easy to make her lose her temper. Edda realized he was pretending not to understand her—and let fly. She said she felt like a prisoner, and so did her husband, and that it was Hitler's duty to set them free immediately. Von Ribbentrop, growing blander as Edda grew more heatedly angry, repeated that there was no reason to leave Almashausen, where Count Ciano could await with his wife, the charming daughter of the Fuehrer's greatest friend, the imminent and inevitable victory of the German forces.

By now Edda had thrown the most elementary caution to the winds. She looked Von Ribbentrop in the face as if she wanted to eat him alive and shouted that the war was already lost—unless they made peace with one of the two enemies, such as Russia, for instance.

Hitler was cut to the quick, and now it was his turn to erupt. "How can you ever mix chalk and cheese," he shouted. "We shall go on fighting against Bolshevism to the last man!"

I made several attempts to take the heat out of the situation—without great success, though everybody quieted down. I begged Von Ribbentrop to look at the matter again as soon as he could, and he gave me a rather vague assurance; in fact, he stubbornly repeated what he had said about the comforts that the Almashausen villa offered the whole Ciano family.

Remembering that day and the cold indifference of Von Ribbentrop, I suspected that when I asked for Edda's children I would now come up against the same wall of excuses and pretenses—and unfortunately I was not to be far wrong. After all, weren't Count Ciano's children perfectly happy staying with my own children and their grandmother in the castle at Hirschberg? Nobody could say they weren't safe or that they were short of anything.

I myself had stayed several times in the castle, and I had to admit that up there it didn't seem like wartime. The castle was about eighty kilometers from Munich and completely impregnable to air attack. It was in an enchanting setting of woods and lakes that teemed with excellent fish. The children had a marvelous time fishing all day, and came back ravenous in the evening.

In this respect too the castle at Hirschberg was an ideal spot, considering the food shortages from which even the children had sometimes suffered. The surrounding countryside provided meat, game, milk, and eggs. My mother, who isn't happy unless she's working in the house, had taken to going down personally into the kitchen to prepare Italian-style meals for us all with pasta, steaks, cutlets, and cake.

The staff who had been assigned to the castle were quick to appreciate the culinary advantages of the situation. They did everything possible to look after the Duce's family; and many of them, if not all, were all the more enthusiastic in the service they gave us because they were able to save some ration coupons and perhaps also take a packet of something home.

All these considerations should have persuaded Edda to give up her plans to have her children back with her in Italy, where they would certainly be worse off than at the castle. But I've always been profoundly convinced that mothers speak a language that is different from that of men or even of fathers, so all I said to Edda was that it was going to be difficult.

"For you," she said putting her arms around me, "nothing's difficult." So I set off for Berlin. I stayed at the Adlon, a magnificent hotel near the Brandenburg Gate, where several members of the diplomatic corps and senior officials of the German Foreign Ministry were also staying. Within hours of my arrival I was asking for an interview with the Undersecretary at the Foreign Ministry; of course I didn't tell him the real purpose of my visit, as I intended to bring it up casually along with several other matters. But my ingenious scheme came to nothing.

Our talk, which took place in a bunker under the hotel while hundreds of English planes were furiously bombing the city, went beautifully until I mentioned Edda's children and her wish to have them back with her in Italy. At that point the German put up the shutters as if an invisible bell had started ringing in his head. He launched with great feeling into a description of the terrible bombardments that Italy was suffering (as if I hadn't experienced them myself) and, on the other hand, the idyllic peace of the castle at Hirschberg. So I had my answer—indirect though perfectly clear— and I realized it would be useless to insist. Saddened by this setback and, above all, worried about its implications, I returned to Italy and told Edda.

"So where are they?" she said as soon as she saw me. I tried to explain that I had had to avoid pressing too hard, because otherwise I would have made the Germans suspicious and they would have become even more rigid, but she wouldn't listen to reason.

"You promised me I'd have my children back, and you've got to get them," she said staring me in the eyes. I don't know why, but I felt embarrassed. I've always been fond of Edda. Sometimes I've been afraid of her, but I've always admired her. Just then my problem was simply not to disappoint her, although I didn't fully realize how important her children were to her; it was almost as if I didn't want to look foolish by showing I was a lesser man than she thought me. And so, a few days later, I set off again for Germany, having made up my mind I would stop at nothing and would ask my father to intervene if necessary. I went with Orio Ruberti, my brother Bruno's brother-in-law and a dear friend of mine. We went in a Lancia Aprilia with a small trailer to take the children's luggage. We set off from Gargnano along the route I had taken many times before—Bolzano, the Brenner Pass, Innsbruck, and Munich. On the way it occurred to me that I would have to change tactics and play for higher stakes. I would have to present my request as if it came direct from the Duce—or I was bound to return empty-handed once again.

In Munich I went to see a senior official of the Foreign Ministry and told him that the Duce wanted the members of his family to return to Italy, the principal reason being that he wanted to reassure public opinion and remove the impression of instability caused by our family still being partly scattered abroad. "Once people see," I told him, "that all the Mussolinis are there with the Duce, there will be a greater feeling of security, something which has never been needed more than now."

This had the desired effect. The official didn't want to take any personal responsibility in the matter, but he assured me he would not stop me doing what I had come to do—he would just pretend to know nothing about it. He very kindly undertook to get me petrol for the journey, and then let me go. A few hours later I had Edda's children in the car—although they didn't like leaving my own children, with whom they played all day and had a whale of a time, nor their grandmother, who had done a great deal for them—and I was back on the road to Innsbruck. I drove flat out and I remember looking around at the children from time to time; it just didn't seem possible that I had been able to do what Edda wanted. We went over the Brenner Pass. Near Bolzano the sirens sounded—just in time for me to stop in the outskirts. Then I and those children, their eyes staring with amazement and terror, watched American Flying Fortresses drop a deadly blanket of bombs over the town. As soon as the enemy planes had flown on over roads devastated by explosions and eerily lit up by raging fires, we left Bolzano and late that evening arrived at the Villa Feltrinelli, Gargnano [Mussolini's last home, on Lake Garda]. Edda welcomed us with joy. She looked at her children, kissed them one by one, then squeezed my hand and said simply, "Thanks, Vittorio."

I had expected her to be more effusive, remembering how she had insisted on having her children back and how contemptuous she had been about my first failure. Not long after, however, I understood everything. Edda's plans to save her husband from being sentenced to death by the Special Tribunal in Verona could have been jeopardized if her three children had remained in Germany exposed to possible reprisal.

With shrewd foresight Edda had wanted first and foremost to get her children out of the Germans' hands and into safekeeping, so that she would be free to act.

By now we were approaching the fatal January 11, 1944, and Edda decided to take the final step. She asked to see my father—it was, if I remember rightly, the day after Christmas. She had already tested the ground in a long talk with my mother, who had tried, to no effect, to make her see that by now not even the Duce's pardon could save Galeazzo from the implacable processes required by the State, and that these were likely to be all the harsher since it was the fate of Mussolini's son-in-law that would demonstrate how firm were the new Republic's laws.

I wasn't present when Edda and my mother had their talk, but I heard about it soon after Edda had stormed out. "It was just terrible," Gina [widow of Bruno, the author's younger brother] told me. "Each of them is fighting to save her own husband and they can't see each other's point of view. There's nothing any of us can do, Vittorio."

Alas, Gina was right. The circle of revolutionary justice was closing remorselessly on the prisoners in the Verona jail. Perhaps it was a question of days, perhaps hours. I realized that nobody could stop what had been set in motion, and I felt an enormous sadness for all of us and for my father, for whom the sacrifice of Galeazzo was the latest and bitterest of the blows the war had dealt him.

But Edda still went on hoping. In her lucid coolness she knew she had only one card in her hand—blackmail—and now was the moment to play it.

So the Germans and the Fascists wanted her husband to die, did they? Well then, let them weigh whether it was better to sentence Galeazzo to death or suffer the consequences of the publication of his diaries. (The Germans attached to the diaries a political importance which perhaps they didn't really have, and in any case they could have no influence on the now inevitable outcome of the war.) There was nothing to hold Edda back. Her children, entrusted to people on whom she could rely absolutely, were already on the point of leaving for Switzerland; the consequences of what she was doing could fall only on herself, free and responsible.

With this desperate form of security, Edda entered the study where my father was awaiting her. I would have wanted to prevent this meeting, which I knew would be terribly painful for both of them, but I arrived too late. Edda had already had confirmation that my father, the man who for more than twenty years had been omnipotent, was bowing before something that was stronger than him. Nothing could stop the judges at Verona from seeing through to the bitter end what they considered their duty. Edda's anger had exploded, heedless of the burning wounds she opened in my father's soul with every word she uttered.

"You're all mad!" I heard her shout. "You're all mad! The war's lost, it's no good deluding yourselves. The Germans will hold out for a few months, but that's all. You know how much I wanted us to win, but there's nothing for it now. Don't you see? And in a situation like this Galeazzo's to be shot!"

For all the fact that during that period I took a line directly opposed to Edda, I am bound to admit that it was difficult to disagree with her. But I took comfort in the conviction that irrespective of how things turned out, we had to keep faith with the ideals for which we had begun our struggle and for which so many had already sacrificed their lives . . . one of them being my brother Bruno.

The door of my father's study burst open, and Edda came out. She was overwrought and shaking, but in her eyes there was an indomitable determination to go on fighting.

"We shall see. We shall see, all right," she said with a measured slowness that scared me. Then she left the villa.

From out in the garden, I heard the happy excited voices of her children playing ball with some soldiers of the Republican Guard.

III

I heard nothing more of Edda after that day I saw her come out, upset and glowering, from my father's study. I was certain my sister would not wait passively for Galeazzo's fate to be sealed, but would fight till the last moment with any means available. What, in practice, she could do I couldn't imagine. I knew the Gestapo had closed in on her and that the SS were watching her all the time. This made me all the more worried, as I knew full well that the more numerous her difficulties and enemies, the more determined and less prudent my sister had always been. And my concern for Edda wasn't the only thought that tormented me during those terrible days.

We had come through 1943, and a new year, a decisive year, was beginning. The forces of the Italian Social Republic were being organized quite fast, and from Germany we were getting fairly reassuring reports on progress with secret weapons. Nevertheless, pressure from the enemy, victorious on all fronts, was building up all the time; and in Italy the specter of civil war was looming all too clearly. Even those who, like myself, had decided that their only course was to fight to the bitter end for the honor of Italy, were bound to be in a state of continual and unnerving tension. Any moment might bring a decisive turn of events. We were all battered by the same storm, and yet each of us still had his own particular agony. I saw mine reflected in the faces of my father and mother, which became more marked with pain and fatigue each day. Edda had disappeared, but we were still aware of her presence and the desperation in which she had turned even against us, as if we were the cruel architects of her plight.

"She'll do something crazy," my mother confided in me. "And then the Germans will have their own back on her. That would finish Papa."

"No, no," I told her, "it'll all sort itself out—you'll see. The Germans are too keen to stop Galeazzo's diaries being published. They'll make a deal. And then Edda and Galeazzo will be all right—and the children too."

My mother listened and then looked at me, saying nothing. She knew I didn't believe it myself, and was only trying to console her. The death sentence for the "Verona Five" was now certain, and it was equally certain that if my father used his authority to impede the course of justice, our newly resurgent Fascism would be dealt a mortal blow and the Germans would immediately take the opportunity to tighten their grip, already terribly heavy, on our benighted country. So the first agonizing days of January went by, and we came to the last act of the tragedy. The Verona judges pronounced the death sentence on De Bono, Ciano, Gottardi, Marinelli, and Pareschi. Sentence was to be carried out at dawn on the eleventh.

It was at two that morning, while the condemned men were awaiting death in the empty, eerie corridors of the Scalzi prison-fortress in Verona, that a German messenger knocked crisply on the door of the chief of the SS in Italy, General Karl Wolff. Wolff answered the door in pajamas, and the messenger, standing stiffly to attention, handed him an envelope. It was addressed to Mussolini and had been deliberately left open.

"If my husband doesn't arrive safe and sound in Switzerland within three days, I shall see that everything is published—which can, as you know, ruin you and the Germans. The diaries are in safekeeping. The proof is irrefutable. Edda."

Wolff put the letter back in the envelope, which he carefully closed and handed back to the messenger, telling him to take it immediately to the Villa Feltrinelli. At that time Wolff was quartered in Fasano, not very far from Gargnano. Edda's last act of defiance, the imminent executions in the Scalzi prison, the agony that my father and the rest of our family were living through—none of this, I think, was of much interest to General Wolff, who for some time from that very villa in Fesano had, behind my father's and Hitler's backs, been laying the basis for a surrender to the Anglo-Americans of all the German forces stranded in Italy. So it was very much in Wolff's interests to appear the most loyal of the Fuehrer's soldiers and the firmest supporter of Fascist recovery, in which the Verona trial was a vitally important element.

"At five o'clock in the morning, an hour before the death sentence was carried out," said Wolff some time later, "my phone rang. It was clear that the Duce had received Edda's letter and wanted to hear my point of view. I reminded him at least twice that Hitler had instructed me not to interfere in the trial, which was something exclusively for the Italian authorities, but the Duce didn't seem very convinced by this. He asked me what I would do in his place, and I could not conceal from him that, given the grave consequences that had stemmed from the vote in the Grand Council and given the popular feeling against those who had signed Grandi's motion, I thought it would be dangerous to grant the pardon for which the condemned men had pleaded. The Duce remained silent for a moment and then asked me what, in my opinion, the Fuehrer was expecting him to do. I sensed I carried a heavy responsibility in my reply, and I hastened to tell him that Hitler doubted the death sentence would be carried out. I knew this would hit home and would clear his mind. The Duce, in fact, was a bit taken aback, but he quickly recovered and asked me what Himmler thought about it. I told him that Himmler, too, was sure that the most severe example should be made. The Duce thanked me and said he would look at the situation again to see if there was some way out."

Wolff has always said he is sure that my father, as soon as he put down the phone, obeyed the dictates of his heart and ordered a stay of execution. I don't know whether that is true. Everything about those last tragic hours is confused, and even the least credible stories can have a grain of truth in them. According to one such story, the Germans themselves had as a last resort made plans for Ciano to escape from the Scalzi prison. The Marchese Emilio Pucci,* who in those days was a most courageous and selfless friend of Edda's, wrote in an article that Galeazzo had on January 3 sent his wife a letter in which he told her that the Germans had decided to free him, no matter what the judges wanted. At nine o'clock on the evening of January 7, Edda was supposed to be at a point ten kilometers from Verona, out on the *autostrada* between Brescia and Verona, where she and Galeazzo would meet and then proceed to Switzerland. This letter was supposed to have been written with the consent of the Germans. But at the same time Galeazzo is said to have sent another letter, via a person he could trust, in which he begged my sister to go straight to Rome to collect, from a hiding place known only to the two of them, several typewritten volumes which contained important notes of meetings with various personalities and which bore the title *Colloqui (Conversations)*; there was another package of even more important documents called *Germania (Germany)*. These were to be the price of his freedom.

At eight o'clock on the evening of January 7, the car in which Edda and the Marchese Pucci were driving

*Later to become famous as a women's fashion designer. He was a pilot during the war, and was twice decorated.

toward Verona broke down. Edda had an hour to get within ten kilometers of Verona, where she was to meet Galeazzo. Pucci stopped a car that was going as far as Brescia, but there was room for one passenger only. Edda climbed in, intent on arriving at all costs. From Brescia she got a lift on a motorbike for a little way, then continued on foot, running in the dark until a passing workman gave her a lift on the crossbar of his bicycle. Edda reached the tenth kilometer stone toward ten o'clock. Nobody was there. Alone and exhausted, she waited hour after hour until five o'clock the next morning. By then the last of her strength had gone. My sister realized she had been tricked once again. She thumbed a lift from a lorry going to Verona, where she waited a few hours at the railway station, exhausted from cold and lack of sleep. Then she gave herself up at the Gestapo post, where she was merely told that "superiors had decided not to free Count Ciano."

A German friend told me, not long afterward, that Hitler had that same day been about to yield to pressures from a number of Nazi leaders who were friends of Ciano's, but that Von Ribbentrop, sworn enemy of my brother-in-law, managed to ward them off.

Edda went back to the clinic at Ramiola where she had been staying, and there received a letter that Galeazzo had managed to smuggle to her. "My Edda," the letter said, "while you are still living under the blessed illusion that within a few hours I shall be free and we shall all be together again, for me the agony has begun. God bless our children. I ask you to bring them up to respect the code of honor I learned from my father and that I could have inculcated into them, had I been allowed to live."

It was the end. As a last desperate act of defiance, Edda decided to flee with the documents to Switzerland, having entrusted to the Marchese Pucci her ultimate threat—the letter to my father which went to him via General Wolff. Then she made herself a belt in which she fixed five of the seven volumes that made up the diary, having first torn off the covers. She tied the belt around her waist under a thick, loose-fitting dress and handed over the other two volumes to a friend at the clinic. The Marchese Pucci pretended to set off for Parma; after a few kilometers he turned cautiously back toward Ramiola along a minor road. In the meantime Edda was pinning on the door of her room a piece of paper on which she had written, "I am very tired and want to rest. Please do not disturb me for any reason whatever." The Gestapo sleuths were unconcernedly eating in the kitchen of the clinic, having seen Edda come in. My sister crept down into the cellars, opened a little door which was used for unloading coal for the boilers, and sped off into the fields. A few minutes later she had climbed into the Marchese Pucci's car and was being driven flat out toward Milan—and thereafter Switzerland.

While Edda was living through this last harrowing part of her adventure, in Gargnano news of the execution of the condemned men was expected any minute. The whole of January 10 passed without news. At dawn on the following day a rumor suddenly went around that the Duce had postponed the execution and called a meeting of his Council of Ministers—probably, it was thought, to order a retrial and thereby save appearances. Word also went around that Hitler had made a personal request to my father to save the condemned men. But these were lies—whether inspired more by mercy or cruelty, I don't know. Late that morning an SS official and one from the Blackshirts came to Gargnano by car and confirmed the news, already received by phone, that a platoon of thirty militia of the Republican Guard had carried out the sentence.

Galeazzo was dead.

Although I had some time before given up all hope for him, and although I knew that the fate of Galeazzo and the other four condemned men was sealed by something stronger than any of us, the news hit me like a thunderbolt. I went instinctively to the Villa Feltrinelli, as if to find refuge. I found my mother ironing in the kitchen. Her eyes were red and her mouth pursed in a painful grimace.

"You've heard," I murmured. "Now it really is all up. Poor Edda."

"Poor Edda," she repeated slowly as she mechanically went on ironing one of Romano's shirts with that meticulous care of hers. Then she shook herself. She looked at me as she used to do when I was a little boy and had done something naughty.

"But what are you doing here?" she said sharply. "Why haven't you been to see your father?"

I hurried away. My father's study, in the Villa delle Orsoline, was only a few steps from where we were living. The time was nearly midday.

Everything around me seemed terribly desolate. At the Villa delle Orsoline I saw a group of officers of the Republican Guard talking in low voices. They recognized me and fell silent, stiffly giving the Roman salute. I knew from their eyes and their silence what they were thinking. A crucial struggle, and a very painful one, had ended two hours before—with the coffins of the Verona Five. Now the way lay open for our last adventure. Fascism was returning to the Social Republican origins from which it had sprung during the hard times of the fierce early struggles—even though hopes of victory were now faint.

I entered the villa. Ministers, undersecretaries, and officers all had a relieved look on their faces as if they had finally seen justice done and yet, at the same time, it was a look that was already overshadowed by a strange regret. My father, they told me, had not wanted to see anybody. I knocked and went in without waiting.

It wasn't a very large room, but had a big window opening onto the lake. My father was sitting by the window, in a low armchair. I looked anxiously at him, searching his face for some sign of recovery. He was shattered. The tension of those last days, brought to breaking point by the tragic hours of that endless sleepless night, the absurd hope of a solution, and the crushing reality of the sentence already carried out—all this had laid him low. He was unshaven. He was still wearing, from the previous evening, his ordinary uniform of the militia without badges or medals, and the collar of his black shirt seemed excessively loose. I went up to him and kissed him, as I always did, trying not to show the emotion that gripped my heart—so that from me, at least, he would have the feeling of a sorrow that I could share and bear with courage.

"Any orders for me this morning, Father?" I managed to say without looking at him. He remained silent for a moment, staring at the lake.

"I've heard," he replied slowly, "that Edda has escaped from Ramiola. She'll probably try to get to Switzerland, where she's already sent her children. The Germans are furious. They've sent at least a hundred sleuths after her from the Gestapo and the SS. We need to find her before they do. If they catch her after what she's done . . . I don't know how it'll end. She's suffered too much already, Vittorio, too much."

I was numbed by an indescribable anguish. I heard again my mother's sharp voice saying, "But what are you doing here? Why haven't you been to see your father?" I thought of Edda, fleeing and pursued by the Germans, and here was my father who was the truest and most tormented victim of the whole tragedy, and I just didn't know what to do. We didn't utter a word for I don't know how long. Then my father pulled himself together with a glimmer of his old vitality.

"What's the general atmosphere like? What are people saying?"

"It's gloomy, Father. Now that Galeazzo and the others are dead, nearly everybody's unhappy and some are already talking about being too severe and saying that bloodshed could have been avoided; but if you had stopped it they would now be ferociously attacking you and accusing you of undermining the dignity of the

Republic to save your daughter's husband, or submitting to the blackmail of Galeazzo's diaries."

"Yes," said my father. "Now they're having regrets. First they're like lions complete with mane, teeth, and claws. They roar as if they could tear man and beast to pieces. And then they eat grass."

He shook his head bitterly. During the last few years his eyes had been progressively opened to a lot of things, and to a lot of men he had blindly trusted and believed, too optimistically, to have superior qualities.

I brought him back to the subject of Edda. I felt that if I shook off inertia and did something, no matter what, I would find some refuge from our sorrow.

"If I leave right away I might catch her at Como. If she really means to go to Switzerland she's bound to go via Como and she'll make a stop at the P. villa. They're the only friends she can trust in that area. If I find her and she gives me the diaries, she can go quietly off to Switzerland—nobody would try to stop her. Don't you think?"

My father agreed with a nod. "See what you can do. If you can manage it, it might be a good thing for all of us. Tell Edda . . ."

He paused as if hesitating to express his feelings. I understood what he meant and I bent over him again to kiss him.

"I'll tell Edda that we all love her, Father. Don't you worry."

My father gave me a long look. "Keep your eyes skinned and don't go alone. Take a good man with you and make sure you're armed. It wouldn't surprise me if some German or some Italian fanatic got on your heels. You never know."

He plucked my cheek in his usual way and turned back to look at the lake again. My father had always, from childhood, had a sort of superstitious fear of lakes.

"They're neither river nor sea," he used to say. "They make me feel they're not to be trusted. I don't know why."

He was sitting looking at the lake which was gray and dismal, under a leaden sky. Across from the window loomed Mount Baldo, covered with snow. Verona was on the other side of that mountain and perhaps, as tradition demanded, somebody there was burning the chairs on which the condemned men had been tied. I couldn't stand it any more. I gave orders to my adjutant to fill up with petrol. Half an hour later I was on my way from the Villa delle Orsoline, driving the same black Aprilia in which, two months before, I had brought Edda's children back from Hirschberg. I drove at high speed through the village streets, which were full of people standing in chilled groups and chatting with black looks on their faces. To be able to drive fast, to have to concentrate on something, though it was only the steering wheel and gear lever of a car, was in itself a great relief and pulled me out of the deadly torpor of that black day. I wasn't even conscious that I was following my sister: I was just intent on getting at all costs on the road she had taken. To catch up with her was the purpose of my mission, but just then it didn't seem to matter at all.

Within a few hours I reached Milan. Then I took the

autostrada to Como. I was conscious that Edda had passed along that road a short time before, and I pictured myself finding her in the P. villa which is a few kilometers from Chiasso. First of all I would want to put my arms around her and say that I was close to her at that terrible time. Then everything would be all right again. There was no more reason for Edda to have the diaries published. Time would soften her anger and she would realize that publication would have only one consequence—it would worsen still further the position of our father and our Government, in favor of the Germans and the anti-Fascists. I was sure I would get the diaries back. Once I had them I would leave Edda at the frontier, and would help her in any way possible to reach safety.

It was dark when I arrived in Como and made my way to the P. villa. I knocked and knocked at the door but nobody came. At last a window opened above me. I said I was Vittorio and asked if they would let me in.

They did so immediately. They seemed genuinely pleased to see me—we were very good friends and I hadn't seen them for over a year—but at the same time they seemed worried about something and afraid to tell me what it was. I became convinced that Edda had stopped at their place, but had already left. We chatted about this and that in a more or less normal way. They too had heard that Galeazzo was dead and were deeply and sincerely sad about it. On some pretext I asked my friends' son, a young man who was a few years older than I, to come out into the garden for a moment. I wanted to talk to him openly about what was weighing on me.

I said immediately, "Where's Edda?"

He tried to hedge. He said he hadn't seen her for a long time, but at the same time he was looking at me in a bewildered way, as if he were afraid I was going to do him some harm. I put my hand on his shoulder and explained the situation in a few words. It wasn't from the Fascists that Edda could be in danger. If anything, it was from the Germans—if they caught her with the diaries on her.

My friend looked at his watch. He seemed to make a quick calculation. Then he looked at me with a relieved expression.

"It's no good my lying to you, Vittorio. Edda's been here, but she left shortly before you arrived. By now she'll certainly be in Switzerland. They can't get her."

So my mission had been a failure and would very likely mean a fresh crop of disasters for all of us. All of a sudden I felt weighed down with the fatigue of that awful day, and with a dark sense of foreboding. Yet there was also a faint absurd happiness. From the dark garden I looked toward Chiesso, glittering with lights like a wonderful mirage. Over there it wasn't dark. Over there people didn't go down into shelters, and men didn't come out of their houses with the fear that they might be shot in the back. Over there was peace, and now Edda and her children could at last live in peace.

But what would my sister do now that she really had nothing more to lose?

I looked spellbound at all that light, and I didn't know the answer. My friend took me by the hand.

"It was better that way, Vittorio," he said affectionately. "Now let's go back in. My parents must be worried."

IV

As many people had foreseen, the execution of the
Verona Five was accepted in the whirl of events as a
painful but unavoidable end of an epoch, making possible an immediate resumption of all the political, military, and social activities of the Republic. Fascism had
demonstrated to Italy—and above all to Germany—
that it could take firm steps no matter what the cost;
and this example, coming as it did directly from the top,
acted as a unifying force. The reconstituted Cabinet
immediately began to function, and interference from
the Germans, though still a difficult and continuous
problem, began nevertheless to be held in check. For
months the front had been stationary at Cassino, and
this too brought a certain reassurance; it seemed likely
that the Allied high command had decided it would be
difficult to advance right up through Italy, where resistance from German troops and the premier divisions of
the Italian Social Republic would be strong and fierce,

and would prefer to switch the real front to the Balkans or (as actually happened) to France.

The problem, it was said, was just one of time, and every day that could be won for the German technicians meant greater hope of winning the secret arms race or finding a political solution to the conflict.

Our family life at the Villa Feltrinelli had returned more or less to normal. We had received news of Edda from Switzerland. She was in a clinic, where she was recovering from a nervous breakdown caused by her tragic loss and the long months that had preceded it. We often thought of her; mixed with the grief we felt for all that had happened to her was the comforting thought that the war could no longer touch her or her children. My father had also regained his health, thanks to fresh treatment from Doctor Zachariae, who had been sent to him by the Fuehrer. My mother continued to look after the house, as always. Romano had begun studying again for his matriculation, and Anna Maria had gone to spend some weeks in a German clinic, about a hundred kilometers from Berlin, where she was being treated for the aftermath of an attack of infantile paralysis she had suffered some years before. It was a military clinic which specialized in the rehabilitation of mutilated and handicapped soldiers. Some real miracles were performed in that clinic, I remember. I had been there once to visit my sister and had come back feeling very hopeful; and I believe that the treatment she had there—happily, a complete course—played a certain part in Anna Maria's return to semi-normality.

Also living at the Villa Feltrinelli were Gina, Bruno's

widow, and her little daughter Marina. I had settled my own wife and children in a villa near Gardone, and when I was in Italy I could see them every day.

My mother ought to have been fairly quiet in her mind, after the recent stormy events. At worst she might have been rather worried about getting enough food for us all, because those were difficult times and my father was stubborn about food rations. Since the outbreak of war his scruples on this subject had been almost absurd. "We must be the first to bear these sacrifices," my father used to say when my mother showed him how little she had been able to buy with her coupons. "You're always the same," she would remonstrate. "We're the only people in Italy who live on their rations. You should see what your ministers eat, and your generals and Party officials."

My father refused to believe it. So then my mother, aggressive and extremely well informed, would give him chapter and verse as to how many kilos of flour went every week to the house of so-and-so, and how many jars of oil she had seen being carried into some other house. "As for us," she would conclude, "we're always the biggest fools." My father didn't know what to say to these quick-fire criticisms which, to the credit of his colleagues, were not always correct. He would look severely at my mother, perhaps hoping to inspire in her a greater respect; but at such moments my mother was first and foremost a Romagnola housewife and wouldn't have been scared of the devil himself. My father, having reaffirmed his principles on the matter, couldn't help taking a suspicious look in the cupboards and pantry, to satisfy himself that, in his house at least, he hadn't been tricked. I remember him one evening standing on tiptoe and running his hand cautiously over the top shelves in the pantry, as if the presence of a couple of ounces of butter or a piece of fat bacon bought on the black market would somehow prejudice the outcome of the war.

I must say that all of us shared his scruples, but within more reasonable limits. My mother, Romano, Gina, and I used to take advantage of Cabinet meetings, when my father was always engaged, to get together and work out our plans for getting provisions. I generally looked after the butter, and Romano the flour, meat, and sausages. It wasn't difficult in those days to find the black market, all the more so as we had countryside all round us. But our problem—and sometimes a worrying one—was money.

I realize that to most people this may seem incredible. A dictator figure is usually associated with unlimited wealth: he can command money at least as easily as he can give an order and see it carried out. In practice things are very different.

In my father's house money was never plentiful. My father was entitled to a considerable salary as a minister and deputy; but he waived it as soon as he came to power, and thereafter he would hear no more of it. He never had a purse or a wallet. I remember that when we, as children, had deserved a present (and naturally we always preferred it in money) he would turn to my mother, and we would get the money from her. She used to eke out very thriftily the fees that came in from the *Popolo d'Italia* [the weekly paper founded in 1914 in Milan by Mussolini, but which he closed down after Badoglio's surrender to the Allies on September 8, 1943], but as is always the case with journalistic work, it didn't provide a regular income. So there were months when my mother in fact found herself short of money, although she knew there was some due to us. This happened especially in the autumn when the newspapers were suffering from the usual summer dearth of advertising revenue and the winter campaigns had not yet got off the ground. At such times my mother used to bring the mealtime conversation around to the North American press agencies and the handsome rates they paid to those lucky enough to work for them.

My father knew what she was getting at, but he used to have fun pretending not to understand. He would answer in general terms, outlining the differences between the North American press and the Italian press. Having a remarkable memory, he would quote the circulations of the biggest American papers, the money spent by the newspaper publishing houses, their advertising revenues, the subsidies which the big trusts found it in their interests to hand out—and he would often dwell on the problem of the freedom of the press in countries with an authoritarian regime. My mother would soon lose patience.

"Benito," she would say very deliberately, "it's time you did some writing." We all used to laugh when my mother said that, especially my father. And often within a couple of hours of leaving the Villa Torlonia he would phone my mother to tell her the article had already been sent off, and she was not to worry. The Americans paid well for those articles; what was more, they paid promptly. And that is the one thing about the United States my mother has always appreciated.

Then, with the founding of the Social Republic and the closing down of the *Popolo d'Italia,* and the fact that for years my father had been unable to contribute to the American agencies, money became a problem again. When my father rose from being head of the government to being head of state, he was once again unwilling to accept the salary offered. But this time he had no choice, and my mother, who had to run the home, found a natural ally in the ministers of the Republic who, as was human and natural, had to pay themselves a salary and therefore pressed my father to do the same. So my father accepted a state allowance—a rather modest one—which, however, he gave up in the autumn of 1944. With so many of us living at home, and the cost of living in those days, I remember it was barely sufficient. There wasn't much left to meet the black-market prices, which became higher and higher every day. But this, alas, wasn't my mother's worst worry, for perhaps the most dramatic moment in her life, certainly the most painful, had arrived.

When my father came back to Italy, Clara Petacci returned to his side. This woman loved my father so much that to be separated from him would have been unbearable for her, especially as he could give her so little time, taken up as he was with the cares of state and his family. So Clara Petacci had moved into a villa in Gardone not far from us.

In a sense the situation was the same as before, if not worse. Politically Clara Petacci's presence on Lake Garda, near my father, was certainly a disadvantage. The Germans—and this was very interesting—seemed to encourage her presence, and so did certain ministers such as Buffarini. They obviously thought that Clara Petacci could have an influence over my father which in fact she herself didn't seek to have and indeed didn't have.

But the really fanatical Fascist Republicans were convinced she wielded this influence—the Badoglio Government's propaganda machine having exploited the scandal—and to them Clara Petacci was a disgrace and a source of danger. They swallowed the story of their leader being twirled around the little finger of a woman who wasn't even his wife, without taking the trouble to find out if it could be substantiated. Even I, in a way, had caught the same disease. I saw this woman as an element in our lives that could have been ignored in normal times but that could be very dangerous in these exceptional circumstances. This was why one morning I decided to risk everything, and I went to see my father at the Villa delle Orsoline to make a clean breast of all my worries and bitterness.

It was one of the very few times that my father and I talked man to man, as equals, with no family or political overtones. I tried to be as calm and logical as possible, but with every word I felt more embarrassed. I told him all that was being said about him and her, and I begged him, for everybody's sake, to sacrifice this woman's love and compel her to leave Gardone as soon as possible.

My father listened to me very seriously, and showed no sign of being annoyed at this interference in his private affairs; and I had the impression that not all I told him was new to him.

His first comment was rather sharp. "With all the difficulties we have to overcome and all we're going through just now," he said as if talking to himself, "there are still people who bother with this tittle-tattle."

From what he said I gathered that he didn't attach overriding importance to his affair with Clara Petacci, and I seized the opportunity to say that if this was the case, it wouldn't be too great a sacrifice to send her away.

My father didn't reply immediately. I had the feeling that, as often happens when a man mature in years and experience talks to a youngster, he didn't consider me yet capable of making a balanced judgment on some situations—as indeed was the case. This was borne out because he went to some lengths to reassure me on the —shall we say—family aspects of the situation, reaffirming that nothing had changed and nothing would change toward my mother and the rest of us.

He talked to me about Clara in a very human way and very calmly, and above all with the respect that any real man owes to a woman, whoever she may be, who really loves him. I was left in no doubt that he had a deep affection for Clara Petacci, perhaps because she was the first woman, among the many he had had, who loved

him without thought of advantage; but I sensed, nevertheless, that she didn't constitute any danger to our
family, and even less was she a political danger. As my
father talked I began to feel smaller and smaller, till I
was not accusing but was accused, all the more so when
he thanked me for what I had said, and then added that,
for his part, he had nothing against sending Clara away
from Gardone.

I left with little feeling of satisfaction at my bitter
victory. Two days later an officer of the Republican
Guard handed me a letter. It was from Clara. I realized
at once that my father had told her everything. In seven
pages of tiny, sensitive handwriting, she rebuked me
for being small-minded in judging a human situation.
That was why, she wrote, I had imagined her love for
my father could be only a source of trouble and petty
dispute.

"I ask nothing from your father and I would have you
know that I would give him anything, including my
life," she wrote. And it wasn't very long, alas, before I
realized that those weren't mere words. In a quieter
tone, with a strength that could only have come from
sincerity, Clara told me that my father lived in an atmosphere of disloyalty and treachery, and that was why
he needed rest and trust above everything.

"Those few hours that we manage to snatch from the
hard reality of men and events," she wrote, "I spend
consoling him for all the painful bitter things. And yet
even you want to send me away. If that proves necessary I shall have to obey. But don't imagine that it
would be an advantage to your father, because if I went

he would be even more alone, with not a single friend —nobody."

At the time her words wounded me: she was accusing me—and this was uncalled for—of lacking in feeling for my father. And yet, as time went by and I thought about it and learned to judge the whole affair in a more human way, I was bound to admit that she wasn't entirely wrong and that a man, at certain exceptional times in his life, cannot always find in his family, among those of his own blood, the comfort that he can derive from a complete outsider, somebody who comes to his side along one of the thousand mysterious paths of love.

But things were coming to a head. My mother had made up her mind, unknown to any of us, to confront her rival and order her to go away. My mother has never been one for half measures. Many women, among them my sister Edda, can fight desperately for their husbands; and of course this is a very noble quality in a woman, because her husband, the father of her children, is her most sacred property. And yet it is one thing if she fights for her husband, and something else if she fights just for her man, irrespective of the fact that the man happens also to be her husband. This may seem a subtle distinction, but it isn't: it points to a whole way of feeling and thinking and living, and it's why women in Romagna say simply, *"E' mi om"* ("He's my man")— meaning "my husband." And in this case my mother was not seeking in the least to exploit her advantageous position as wife and mother, at the expense of her rival. Woman she was and woman she wanted to remain—a woman in love and yet jealous and determined to fight to the end. She might hide her jealousy behind warnings of dire political dangers—for politics also ran in her blood—but she would still face the situation with realism and courage. She knew that in the end she had always won, even against women who had been able to offer my father beauty, sensitivity, culture—all vastly superior to her passionate but primitive devotion.

On this occasion my mother fought in the same way as she had always done, confident she would come out on top. The meeting, in Clara Petacci's villa, was dramatic, almost desperate. At the end of it neither had shifted her ground, which was to be expected, although on the face of it my mother had had some success because Clara, distraught, decided to leave.

It was to be only a temporary success and bought at a high price. For the first time my mother had come up against somebody who could fight with the weapons she used herself—those of a total love. A crisis was inevitable. For the first time in my life—apart from the days following the births of Romano and Anna Maria —I saw my mother confined to her bed, struck down by a terrible nervous shock. The doctors were worried, fearing a breakdown. For my father, who had immediately heard by telephone from Clara about the violent clash, the shock was almost as great. All day he kept telephoning, as he was afraid my mother wouldn't want to see him. Then, toward evening, he sent her a note asking if he could come. My mother, I remember, brightened up and, with innocently feminine tactics, charged me to tell Papa that she would willingly see him, but a bit later. In the meantime she tidied the room and freshened herself up a bit. She was overwrought and exhausted—an unrecognizable wreck.

My father soon arrived, upset and distressed. I brought a chair to my mother's bedside and left them alone in the hope that they would find an hour's peace. They stayed together the whole evening. From the next room, from which I couldn't tear myself away, I could make out only a few words; it was my father who talked nearly all the time, in his grave, warm voice.

I gathered that, little by little, they found their true selves again in their reminiscences—of the tough but happy years of their love, from that faraway afternoon in November 1909 when my father went to her home to take her away with him. What was my father then? A revolutionary, with hardly a penny to his name, whom people listened to as if he were a prophet and whom the police watched like a dangerous subversive. A restless daunting man: when my mother took the liberty of dilly-dallying over his peremptory demand to follow him, he pointed a revolver and announced he would exterminate her and all the family and then kill himself.

So she followed him, and for years she had been his brave, loyal companion, keeping in the background when things were going well and returning to his side as soon as there was more fighting and suffering to face. Marriage itself, which for nearly all women in the world is an essential guarantee of security and, as such, is the only tie that justifies complete dedication, was for my mother a mere formality which she eventually accepted only because by then my father's position made it necessary; but up to then she had not wished to hear of it.

"You don't hold a man with a stamped certificate," she used to say—and I am bound to admit that in a sense she was right.

But now, at the door of her own house, was a danger that could not be driven away with either certificates or her devotion. The problem was to know whether her man really had stopped loving her because of another woman.

That evening my mother sensed with her deep intuition that she hadn't lost my father. Certainly it was a terribly difficult situation, but perhaps it would pass like all the others. She gained faith from my father's great tenderness and the way he stayed at her bedside, so humbly and with such genuine affection.

My mother has always been a practical woman, has always taken things a step at a time. That evening she knew for sure that, for a start, the other woman was going to move away, and my father was not lost. This was enough to enable her to go on fighting as soon as her strength allowed.

Two days later my mother was on her feet again, working in the house just as before—in fact, more so. I was about to set off again for Germany; I had packed my bags and was waiting for the car. I took a stroll in the garden of the Villa Feltrinelli with my mind on nothing in particular and almost at peace with myself, when I suddenly spotted my mother climbing over a low wall and down a bank. I knew that wild lettuce

grew there—something my father was very fond of—
and I found myself smiling. I steathily climbed over the
wall and came up behind her.

"Ah, ha," I said, "what are you doing here?"

She realized in a flash that I meant to tease her, and
she gave me a cross look.

"I'm getting some wild lettuce. Didn't you know
your father liked it?"

"And you've fallen for it again," I said. "You've been
shouting and screaming for thirty years. Then he
comes and pays you a few compliments, and you swallow the lot and go running off to get him some wild
lettuce."

My mother put one hand into the apron in which she
was holding the wild lettuce, as if to hold on to it
tighter.

"You Mussolinis," she retorted, "you're all the
same."

Then she started laughing and stooped again to
search slowly in the grass.

V

Ever since the news that Edda had crossed the frontier into Switzerland, safe from any sort of reprisal, we had daily been expecting some dramatic development. Galeazzo had paid the penalty demanded by law, and the publication of the diaries which my sister had tried up to the last minute to barter for her husband's life could not bring him back from the dead. Yet, we were practically certain that Edda would lose no time in having the diaries published, merely in order to carry out her threat. Besides, she had promised she would do it, before she left Italy, and we knew that too short a time had elapsed for the effects of the recent agonizing events to have started wearing off. Those whose job it was to tune in to Swiss and Anglo-American stations were told to listen for anything concerning my sister. From time to time they reported hearing brief news of her: she was slowly regaining her health, and she never went outside the clinic where she was staying with her children. But that was all. Ciano's diaries could already have been in every bookshop in the Western world, had Edda wished it; yet it seemed as if they had never existed.

That was all years ago, and I am certain now that Edda acted as she did for the sake of my father—even though at that tragic time she had judged him to be her enemy and had told him so and deeply hurt him. Perhaps she had even hated him. For Edda there are no intermediate stages between love and hate, but she is also a woman of great common sense and fairness. Anyway, the diaries came out in New York in 1945, when my father was dead and the war had been lost.

It was illogical and generous—and typical of her. But it would take a massive volume to explain why she acted in that way, and indeed to explain many other disconcerting things she has done. Few women of our time have had a more eventful and dramatic life. Few women have been more talked about than she has, both in her heyday and even now—talked about (as often happens in these cases) with a minimum knowledge of the facts, a maximum amount of pure fantasy, and, I would add, much bad taste. But this may stem from the fact that when someone is difficult to understand, the temptation to fabricate stories about that person is too great. And if, on top of that, advantage is taken of the swing of political fortunes by virtue of which only the victorious side is entitled to write history, the result is calumny and gratuitous insults. For me there is nothing mysterious about Edda—and I can claim to know her well because we are united by a deep affection.

When I was born, on September 28, 1916, my sister was in her first year at school. She was born on September 1, 1910, and from the very beginning she had, albeit unwittingly, been placed in a very odd position. Malicious gossip can throw doubt on a child's paternity. But, as the song says, there can be only one mother. For Edda it was the other way about. For years and years, despite all the evidence of our family life and especially of my mother (who, I would have thought, was the person most closely concerned), the tale of Edda as the daughter of a famous father and an unknown mother has continued to circulate in the salons and newspapers of the world. Even in February 1945, when nations on both sides were making their supreme military effort, a Swiss paper came out with the great revelation that Edda was not my mother's daughter. And I remember that my father, although more than thirty years had passed since the first innuendos, was filled with a new bitterness; my mother, on the other hand, didn't deign to give the paper so much as a glance. I can dispense with this matter, which is so absurd that it can't really harm us, by producing one piece of evidence: the behavior of my mother. It is enough to have met my mother once to realize that some other woman's daughter would never have come into *her* house. My mother isn't a character out of a nineteenth-century novel, a woman who could have borne such a cross and pretended for the rest of her life. There were times when jealousy made her furious with my father, and I heard her accuse him of the most trivial things; and it's obvious that, had she possessed a weapon as strong as an illegitimate daughter, she would have used it on those occasions. Yet, it's worth adding a rider here, because every story, no matter how incredible, has a grain of apparent truth which therefore makes it believable.

The story is that Edda is the daughter of a Russian Jewess, and "informed sources" have named Angelica Balabanoff. It is perfectly true that Angelica Balabanoff and my father knew each other—and intimately. They met in Switzerland, where the Russian Jewess, who was some fifteen years older than my father, was a leading personality in international revolutionary circles. Angelica Balabanoff took a great liking to my father—and there is no doubt at all that the political fighting spirit of his unconventional temperament was not the only thing she admired about him. Helped by Angelica Balabanoff, my father managed to live by doing translations from the German, a language of which he then had only a scanty knowledge but which she knew extremely well. At the same time Angelica Balabanoff tried to influence him toward Marxism, knowing full well that he would have been a very valuable convert to her political cause. When my father returned to Italy, she followed him and worked with him on *Avanti!* [the Italian Socialist Party newspaper] until the campaign in support of Italy's intervention in the First World War. My father and mother and Edda then lived at 18 Via Castelmorrone, and Angelica Balabanoff at No. 9 on the same street. Every evening my father and the Russian Jewess took the same route back from the newspaper office, and often they would stop for some time together. So it was, probably, that the rumor originated that Edda was Angelica Balabanoff's daughter, although at the time Edda was already at least four years old. And all this is in spite of the fact that Angelica Balabanoff herself has spoken out in her book, published in clandestine editions of *Avanti!*, whose very title *(The Traitor Mussolini)* gives an idea of how well-disposed she was to my father.

"He was accompanied," runs one passage in the book, "by a quiet, humble submissive woman and an undernourished little girl wearing a transparent dress which had been soaked by the heavy rain. 'This is my friend Rachele and my daughter,' he said, introducing them. The sight of those two pathetic creatures made me feel angry with Mussolini. . . ."

What is more, an old Socialist, Ugo Barni, as well as many others who were living in Forli in 1910, knew my mother when she was expecting Edda. Someone else who would be able to recall things that were said in confidence by my father, as well as visits from my mother with the newborn Edda in her arms, is Pietro Nenni, the former leader of the Socialist Party. Both my father and Nenni went to prison for fomenting the general strike against the war in Libya. My father had made an extremely violent speech at a socialist meeting, at the end of which he had called on the women to lie down on the railway tracks to prevent the troop trains from leaving. "We shall see whether they are prepared to run over the mothers and wives of our soldiers," my father shouted, and the crowd, already in those early days completely dominated by his magnetism, went rushing to the station, smashing everything in its way.

Nenni, who at that time was head of the Republican Party of Forli, had also incited people to stop the troop trains leaving. The police, who could not hold out against the demonstrators, instead took it out on him and my father. Nenni and my father shared the same cell. Though they had been political adversaries up to then, they became the best of friends. Nenni's wife used to visit my mother and Edda, and together they would share the little money (and the many troubles and hopes) they had in those difficult times. On visiting days my mother would go with little Edda and Nenni's wife to see the two prisoners, taking the few packets allowed by prison regulations, as well as lots of papers, which were forbidden—because by this time the two women knew all about prisons and could take in and bring out whatever they wanted. The friendship between the two men, founded on shared ideals, but above all on mutual esteem, lasted for more than ten years, and one proof of it is the fact, which today seems almost incredible, that Pietro Nenni was godfather to both me and Bruno. Edda, at the time, was six years old—not old enough to reason, but already old enough to sense things; and what she had already come to prize most were the privileges, few because of poverty but no less important for that, of being an only child.

The idea of another child being born—and one with whom she would have to share these privileges—was a nightmare to Edda. She felt she would have to give up something precious: her parents' affection, particularly that of her father and her father's friends—people from that strange world of revolutionaries, journalists, painters, and dreamers, associated with café tables full of smoke and polemics, benches in filthy, noisy printing works, Interventionist meetings which were often broken up by charging mounted police. Edda, hanging on to my father's trousers, running to keep up with the adults so as not to be a nuisance and not to be left out, was absorbing that atmosphere day and night, and she enjoyed a complete and special relationship with my father—a thing of fascination that could not and should not be shared with anybody. The Via Castelmorrone, in those days, was in the outskirts of Milan. We had a couple of rooms on the top floor, the fourth—my father never wanted to be lower down because he couldn't stand neighbors' footsteps above him. It was a big crumbling block of flats, full of people as poor as us and even poorer. Edda was always out in the street, playing with the other children, and my mother used to shout at her for getting lice in her hair.

My maternal grandmother lived with us; she was a tall, thin old lady who worked all day and had a boundless admiration for my father—to such an extent that she nearly always sided with him against my mother.

In that strange home, where there was probably a lavatory but certainly not a bath—because all the time we were there, we children were always taken to the municipal showers—there had lived, since a few days before I was born, another character who had assumed great importance: a cockerel. It had been sent to us from Romagna in anticipation of the happy event. But, as often happens with happy events, calculations had gone wildly wrong, and though I arrived precisely on time, everybody thought I was late. So the cockerel was allowed to live, and within a few days had made itself perfectly at home, getting fatter and more full of itself all the time. To Edda that cockerel was a marvelous toy. She used to take it around all the time, feed it, stroke it, talk to it, and tease it. But when I came into this world, the cockerel had to be dispatched into the next. My grandmother sent Edda out on some pretext, got hold of the cockerel, and wrung its neck. My mother got some chicken soup, but my sister got the cruelest shock of her childhood. Now, all these years later, Edda and I talk gaily about those far-off days, and she admits that, at the time, she hated me with all her strength. It was for me that her cockerel had been sacrificed and, almost as if that weren't enough, everybody in the block came up to see me and coo over me. It was just too much, and there grew up in my sister's mind, spontaneously and very vividly, the desire to kill me. These are terrifying words, but they reflect something which is entirely normal in such cases. In all families the firstborn suffer, more or less intensely, from such complexes.

Having tested the ground in a whole series of minor skirmishes, not the least of which was an attempt to get milk from my mother so that I wouldn't be the only one to be nursed by her, Edda one day took decisive action.

It was my grandmother's habit, when I had been fed by my mother, to hold me so that I digested the milk. She would come out of my mother's room and into the kitchen, rocking me, and then sit down by the range. It was then that, one day, my sister with the speed of

lightning kicked away the stool on which my grandmother was about to sit down with me in her arms. My
grandmother fell with a shout—and she fell all the
more heavily because she kept her arms around me, to
save me, and couldn't put out her hands to break the
fall. My grandmother realized what lay behind my sister's action, and I am sure she suffered more from that
knowledge than from her fall, which, by the way, didn't
injure her at all seriously. She got up, put me on the
bed, and then came back into the kitchen and taught my
sister the lesson she deserved. Just then my mother
came in, holding me under her arm like a bundle: She
took stock of the situation, handed back to my grandmother my small and uncomprehending person, and
administered a second dose of smacks to Edda. From
then on Edda made no more attempts on my well-
being! Besides, it wasn't long before there was more
talk of babies, because my mother was expecting
Bruno. Bruno was born eighteen months after me, in
April. He was the only one not to be born in September, as the rest of us all were—Edda, myself, Romano,
and Anna Maria. It's a coincidence that we have chaffed
my parents about from time to time.

With Bruno on the scene, my sister decided it was
better to try to come to an understanding with the
newcomers. For all three of us this problem came up
again in 1927 when Romano was about to be born. We
were already quite grown up and we expressed our
disapproval, on the day of the happy event, by giving
our collective judgment on our new brother—"He's so
ugly. He looks like a monkey." But a year later we

realized that our parents were incorrigible, because Anna Maria was born. We decided that the best thing would be a general alliance, between all five of us, when the two smallest were old enough to play. Edda remained the accepted head of the group, as she had always been.

Edda, Bruno, and I had in the early days called ourselves "The Three Musketeers" from the film of the famous novel. Then our tastes changed. After Dumas it was the turn of Salgari [a popular adventure writer of the day], and we gave ourselves the names of heroes from his books. Even now my sister sometimes calls me Yanez and I call her Sandokan. We always remained keen on Salgari, even when we were reading other authors. Like all children in those days, we devoured the comics with stories of Nick Carter, Petrosini and, above all, Lord Lister the gentleman thief, but in this we earned the lively disapproval of my mother, who thought she was far above us because she read an extraordinary publication, *Sonia, or the Martyr of the Russian People*, which came out in installments that were half the size of a newspaper and full of naïvely dramatic drawings. I've always thought that *Sonia* must have made quite a lot of money for her publisher because the story went on and on, just like the Jane and Superman cartoons of today's American newspapers; and the installments built up to incredibly thick volumes.

Edda, willful, brave, and resourceful, was not only the natural leader for me and Bruno but also for the other boys and girls of the neighborhood. We used to play in the public gardens and in what is now called the

Piazzale Marengo; and sometimes—but this was a game in which we allowed only certain friends chosen for their prowess and contempt for danger—we played on the roof of our block. The roofs and skylights were our Dolomites, and the *cordata* [a roped party of mountaineers] was our great joy—all the more intense in that it was so dangerous. It was Edda who invented it. We would take turns to sit astride the roof, holding on to the chimney with one hand and giving the other hand to the next child, who gave his free hand to the next, and so on till the last of us could lean out over the gutter. What there was to be seen that couldn't be seen from a window, of course, we couldn't say; but that counted for nothing compared with the sense of having done something that was, first and foremost, severely forbidden and, second, very brave.

Only when we grew up and could have a truer idea of the value of life and one's duty to preserve it, did we realize what folly the game had been. But at the time we couldn't see that.

My father, who had a dislike for private schools, decided we should enroll at State schools, where we would be in touch with working-class children. So we began our student lives at the elementary school in the Via Palermo, while Edda went to high school at the *ginnasio liceo Parini*, in the Via Fatebenefratelli. My sister started at the Parini on October 16, 1920. My father paid the eighteen-lire enrollment fee and another twenty-five lire for the first installment on the school fees. Edda figures in the school register of that date as number twenty-six in the list of girl pupils for the first high-school year, section G. Although she was a terror —thin, pale, and restless—Edda got through her exams with good marks. For many years my parents kept Edda's school report for the year 1921–22: she had 7 and 7 [out of 10] in Italian, 8 and 7 in Latin, 8 in history, 7 in geography, 8 in French, 7 and 7 in math, 10 in physical education (the only mark she was proud of), and 8 for conduct. The teachers all said Edda was a clever girl, but they regretted the fact that, because of her temperament, she couldn't produce the results that her exceptional intelligence merited. Her childhood, especially the early years, had played a decisive part in the formation of this temperament.

"I remember," Edda once told a scandalized group of ladies, "I used to go barefoot into the country with my mother to get vegetables. My clothes were all torn and I was always starving hungry. I've never known the middle areas of life: from the very bottom I shot to the very top, all at once. I was a bundle of rags, and now I'm one of the best-known women in Europe."

The truth is that those early days were full of privations and adventures. My father had devoted himself to politics, which was the reason why he regularly ended up in prison a few days after he had been released. There were no openings for him, except occasional work for newspapers, which were often, in any case, suppressed even before contributors could be paid. It was only in Forli, when the Socialists founded the weekly *La lotta di classe (The Class Struggle)*, that my father could count on a salary. The president of the town's Socialist Party branch proposed to the Assembly the nomination of Benito Mussolini as editor of the new weekly, with a salary of 150 lire a month. The Assembly, which was very well disposed to my father, approved the proposal and was concerned only to ensure that there were sufficient funds to guarantee the salary: this was to be achieved by the *Camera del Lavoro* [Trade Union movement], the Party branch and the newspaper each contributing fifty lire. Everything would have gone swimmingly if my father, putting as always his political prestige before his own interests, had not turned it down flat.

His friends were amazed, and they protested. They reminded him he had a woman and a little girl to keep, and they all brought up the fact that, as my father was not married and had not baptized his daughter, he was all the more entitled to Socialist support. After a long argument my father accepted 120 lire, which was very little, especially when the expenses of his political life were taken into account. Soon after that he moved to Milan to become editor of *Avanti!* My mother stayed behind alone with my sister in Forli, where Socialist friends helped her as best they could. My mother helped in their houses, washing, ironing, and making bread. Edda gave her a hand when there was a lot to do, and spent the rest of the time wandering about the streets and fields.

But when finally my father was able to arrange for his family to join him in Milan, times were still almost as hard, at least until *Il Popolo d'Italia* was founded. Then my parents' lives became easier or, to be more exact, less poverty-stricken, and my mother no longer had to go from house to house trying to earn a few lire. But that didn't mean Edda was growing up in a quieter atmosphere. Bruno and I were still small, so Edda was on her own.

She dominated everything around her, the other children and even her own father, whom she sometimes answered back with unsuspected arrogance. But she certainly didn't have a happy childhood: some dark force—the weight of poverty, suffering, and anxiety that had lain on our family—continued to separate her from other children.

There had already been an example of this at the high school. A second example, and the decisive one, was to come a few years later when my father decided to send her to boarding school. By then many things had changed both for our family and for our country. My father had come to power, and we had moved to Rome to live in the Villa Torlonia. Ours was a stormy arrival: my mother found a maid, a certain Cesira Carrocci, who didn't suit her at all. Perhaps it was because she was rather too pretty, perhaps because she was not very submissive in her manner, feeling that she was protected by my father. Anyway, the sacking was inevitable. Cesira protested to my father, who asked my mother why she thought it necessary to get rid of this woman who had up to then done her work very well.

"I don't like the woman," my mother replied fiercely, "and that's that. You're in charge of Italy, but here in my house I'm in charge. That woman's got to go."

My father, like a good husband, didn't push the point any further, and Cesira packed her bags.

Edda was growing up in years, but outwardly she was no young lady. Without being in any way coquettish, she went on wearing the simplest little dresses: all she wanted was something in which she could run and jump and climb like a boy. Other girls of her age were mad about stockings, but she wore short socks, was proud of the scratches and bruises on her legs, and made remarks about "those stupid girls who think they're already women." My father and mother were worried, all the more so as our family had now come up so rapidly in the world. The problem of giving a more refined upbringing to their eldest child, with a future husband also in mind, could not be deferred any longer. And so, after many arguments, they decided to send Edda to Florence to attend the Poggio Imperiale College where, a few years previously, Princess Maria Jose, the future Queen of Italy, had been a pupil. The registers of that college contained the finest names from the world's aristocracies. The daughters of kings, princes, and millionaires from all over the world were sent to the Poggio because it was thought that, apart from a mastery of the purest form of Italian, the girls would also have the advantage of making new acquaintances of the highest rank—something that would be useful for their future role in high society. My parents probably didn't realize how dangerous such a drastic change of environment would be for Edda. She was fifteen and an incorrigible tomboy, likable but seeming unlikely to acquire more polished ways. Already on one occasion she had with complete naturalness (and, I must say, justification) called a *prefetto* [head of local government] an imbecile when he kissed her hand during a reception. What would happen when she was suddenly thrown into the cream of the world's most sophisticated young ladies, God alone knew. It wasn't long before we knew too. Alarming reports began to reach us from Florence. She had hardly set foot in the college before she called the headmistress (Maria Patrizi, from one of the finest aristocratic families in Florence) a hairy old witch.

In spite of the discreet arrangements my father had made for keeping an eye on her, Edda found a way to correspond with the girls she considered her only real friends—schoolmates from the Parini in Milan. There were two in particular, Anna Scaglia and Anita Perrone, who understood her and were fond of her, putting up with her faults and admiring her good points. For several months Edda toyed, in letters to these friends, with the idea of escaping from the college, where she sensed all too well that she was tolerated only because she was the daughter of the Duce. But it must have been Edda herself who realized there wasn't much chance of her plan succeeding, and so with deep regret she gave it up.

"Dearest," she wrote to one of the friends, "I'm so pleased you remember me. You can't imagine how much one lacks affection here. All one asks is a kind word, and not the false piety so fashionable here at the Poggio Imperiale, but it's not to be had. I'd just love to come back to your class and put it right or suffer the consequences with you all if we failed. Your plan for me to escape is well thought out and wouldn't be wicked, but I can't do it. If I were just anybody, I'd do it in a flash, but I'm a Mussolini. So I can't—it's maddening!"

So thought my sister when she was fifteen. But the whole question of Edda's education and upbringing was soon to seem of little moment compared with some other inevitable problems—ones which were more delicate and, given Edda's lively temperament, more fraught with danger, at least in the opinion of my parents.

For my sister was already grown up and had reached that strange and marvelous age that we all remember in our lives. The age when we fall frequently in love.

September 13, 1943. The Duce stepping from the Junker aircraft which had brought him to Hitler's General Headquarters. Some hours earlier he had been freed by German commando troops, led by Captain Otto Skorzeny, from a hotel prison on a mountain top in the Gran Sasso, a ski resort in the Apennines. Here his son Vittorio joyfully greets him, while a smiling Führer looks on.

The garden of Hirschberg Castle, near Munich, where many members of the Mussolini family stayed for some weeks after September 8, 1943 (the day when Marshal Badoglio's government surrendered to the Allies and three days before the Germans seized Rome). Photo shows the Duce, his wife Rachele, and Vittorio Mussolini's children, Guido right and Adria. In this same castle Rachele Mussolini looked after Count Ciano's three children before they were whisked back to Italy by the author, at their mother's request. (See Chapter 3.)

Spring 1944 at Gargnano on Lake Garda. The Italian leader, his health greatly improved, goes for a bicycle ride along the paths in the garden of the Villa Feltrinelli, where the Mussolini family lived during the 600 days of the Italian Social Republic (the Saló Republic). Behind him is the big window that looks on to the lake.

Clara Petacci, Mussolini's mistress, in 1938.

Berlin, 1938. Countess Edda Ciano (the author's sister) at a reception given in her honor by Goebbels.

Mussolini at his desk in the Villa delle Orsoline, Gargnano, Lake Garda, about to broadcast a radio message. To his right, giving advice, is Daquanno, of the Ministry of Popular Culture (propaganda). Left: Ferrando Mezzasoma, who was in charge of that Ministry. Both Daquanno and Mezzasoma were shot by partisans at Dongo on April 28, 1945. (Mussolini and Clara Petacci were shot—machine-gunned at almost point-blank range—on that same day.)

Cattolica (in Mussolini's native region of Romagna), 1925. Mussolini and daughter Edda on the beach. (See Chapter 6.)

*Verona, January 1944. The Special Tribunal in session at the trial
of the signatories of Grandi's motion of July 25, 1943, which
brought about the downfall in Rome of the Fascist regime.
From left: Marshal Emilio De Bono (head in hands), one of the
Quadrumvirate that commanded the early Fascist militia; Carlo
Pareschi, one-time Minister of Agriculture; Count Galeazzo Ciano,
one-time Foreign Minister and one-time Italian Ambassador to the
Holy See (and the author's brother-in-law); Tullio Cianetti,
one-time Minister of Corporations; Giovanni Marinelli, one-time
Treasurer of the National Fascist Party; Luciano Gottardi, one-
time President of the Confederation of Industrial Workers. All
save Cianetti (sentenced to 30 years' imprisonment) were executed
by firing squad on January 11, 1944.*

*Gargnano, Lake Garda, 1944. The Duce leaving the Villa
Feltrinelli to a "present arms" from a member of the Republican
Guard left, and a soldier of the SS.*

Winter 1916. Corporal Benito Mussolini of the 11th Bersaglieri, on a few days' leave from the Carso Front, sees his first born son, Vittorio, pictured here in the arms of Rachele Mussolini. The future Duce has his hand on the shoulder of his daughter Edda, then seven. (See Chapter 5.)

Mussolini's family soon after the March on Rome, October 28, 1922 (as a result of which the Fascists seized power). From left: Edda, Signora Mussolini, Bruno and Vittorio (in sailor suit).

*The Villa Torlonia (the Mussolini family residence in Rome),
April 1930. The Fascist leader and head of the Italian government
awaiting with his daughter Edda the arrival of guests at the
reception for Edda's marriage to Count Galeazzo Ciano.
(See Chapter 6.)*

The bride and groom making their way (after their marriage at the Church of San Giuseppe) to St. Peter's, Rome, in accordance with an old Roman tradition whereby newlyweds must kiss the feet of a bronze statue of the Apostle.

London, about 1938. Guglielmo Marconi pays his respects to Countess Edda Ciano at the reception given in her honor. Center: the wife of the Italian Ambassador in London, Dino Grandi (it was Grandi who in July 1943, in the Fascist Grand Council, put the motion that led to the arrest and imprisonment of Mussolini).

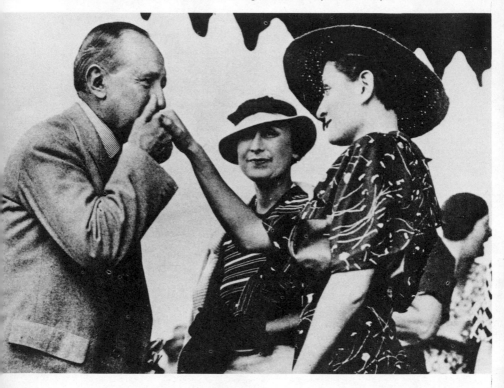

Rome, 1960, in church at a relative's wedding. From left: *Maria Teresa Baccherini (daughter of the Duce's sister Edvige), Rachele Mussolini, Edda Ciano, and Donna Carolina (Galeazzo Ciano's mother).*

Edda Ciano taking part in a Red Cross ceremony on the Greek Front, 1941.

Predappio (the Commune in Romagna where Mussolini was born),
August 30, 1957. At last Mussolini's corpse is handed over to his
family, twelve years after his death. Standing sorrowfully by the
wretched coffin that contains the Duce's remains and is covered
with a tricolor drape and many flowers, are from left: Count Vanni
Teodoràni-Fabbri (with moustache) and his wife Rosa (wearing
glasses), daughter of Arnaldo Mussolini, the Duce's brother;
Countess Edda Ciano; Commendator Augusto Moschi, cousin of
Rachele Mussolini; Marzio Ciano; Rachele Mussolini; Raimonda
Ciano; Romana Montanari, daughter of a cousin of Rachele
Mussolini who was shot by the partisans; Romano Mussolini, the
Duce's youngest son. Unable to attend were Vittorio Mussolini,
who was in the Argentine, and Anna Maria Mussolini, who was ill.
(Anna Maria died in 1968, at the age of only forty, and lies in the
same family tomb as her father, at San Cassiano, Predappio.)

The Villa Carpena, Forlì, home of Rachele Mussolini. The eighty-first birthday (April 10, 1971) of the Duce's widow being celebrated with a family party. There are 81 candles on the cake. Countess Ciano has her hand on her mother's shoulder. Son Vittorio watches as the old lady, still with all her mental and physical faculties, puts out the candles.

A print showing Rachele Mussolini at the age of eighty.

VI

I have to smile at the story of my sister falling in love
with the stationmaster from Cattolica. In those days, in
the summer of 1925, I wasn't a confidant of Edda's—at
least not in affairs of the heart—which is natural, because whereas a difference of six years counts for practically nothing between adults, it is a great gulf between
a girl who is already a young woman and a boy who is
still a child. All the same, I began to understand that my
sister might have certain personal interests other than
our games. But one thing I must say very clearly is that
I got to hear of this and many other stories from reading
newspapers during the period of the Badoglio Government and the early postwar years. And I would call the
journalists who wrote them, judging by the way they
reported events of which I was an informed and direct
witness, fantasy merchants to say the least. Edda had
many boyfriends and girlfriends, as is perfectly natural
for any girl of fifteen who, when school is over, goes off

to the seaside. And since I can only remember seeing her go out with boys and girls who were older than the rest of us, I can't rule out the possibility that among them there might have been the "famous" station-master.

But I still maintain that if something important really had happened, Bruno and I, innocent little lads that we were, would sooner or later have got to know about it, if only because of the fuss my mother would probably have made . . . and in this respect she never had anything to complain about. It would have been a serious problem, on the other hand, for my father. I must say that, in his scrupulous concern to give, through his family, an example to the whole country, he kept a discreet eye on everything we did, and when he couldn't do so himself he used his informants. And this, quite frankly, was tiresome, even though we had the comfort of knowing we weren't doing anything wrong and therefore had nothing to fear from him. So it is probably true that through this network of infor-mants—and I don't know how intelligent or honest they were—a number of reports began that year to land on my father's desk in Rome while my sister and the rest of us were peacefully and contentedly enjoying our summer holidays.

Thinking back on all this today with absolutely no animosity, but only in the light of good sense and what I can remember—which includes nothing remotely like the story circulated—I can give only one explanation: either it was a stupid excess of zeal or, which is perhaps more likely, a small but poisonous vendetta of political origin, directed at my father through his personal family life.

Whatever it was, my father was worried. My mother, who was directly responsible for family affairs, tried to make her husband understand there was nothing to worry about. But he was immovable. This little flirtation had to end—and immediately. He had enough worries in Rome, without having to waste time with the Chief of Police on reports of a stationmaster's movements. In his understandable but sometimes excessive concern with public opinion my father took the radical decision to post the young stationmaster to Sicily, not realizing that by this measure, which was out of all proportion to the real situation, he was ensuring that rumors, including the most absurd and vicious, would fly all the thicker. I believe that to Edda, not seeing the stationmaster (if he ever existed) any more was neither here nor there. What perhaps did hurt her was to be treated as if she had really let down the family, when she knew she had done nothing wrong.

That is the only light I can throw on this matter which, according at least to the newspapers I read in the early postwar years, had its brief moment of importance in Italian gossip. And I'm amazed that those newspapers, which were supposed to be so well informed, forgot one rather interesting detail—which is that Edda had a proposal of marriage when she was in her second year at primary school.

At the time we were living in Milan, in the Via Castelmorrone. The precocious suitor was in the fourth year and lived on the floor below ours, with his mother and a sister. "The mother," Edda has recorded, "was a well-preserved woman who used to make the table jump when she evoked the spirit of her dead husband, and the sister was a good-looking girl of about twenty to whom my father gave lessons in pure mathematics (lessons which were soon ended because my mother didn't believe they served any useful purpose). I remember that little boy well. He was a bit bigger than me and was the first one to say, 'When I grow up I'll marry you.' He used to give me lots of presents. He had fixed up a sort of cable car between his window and mine, and the presents arrived by air. I remember, among other things, lots of balls of colored wool. Although I've forgotten the face that used to look up at me, I can still see those colored balls slowly ascending, suspended in mid-air. Of course he had stolen them from his mother. I didn't ask for anything; it was all given out of pure love. His joy in giving didn't move me, nor did I get any particular joy out of receiving, but the precarious bobbling of those colored balls was marvelous, and so was the fear that any moment they might plunge down into what to me seemed an abyss. . . ."

After that little lad, another remarkable character figures in the records of my sister's "conquests," a boy we have all of us always called Fiumano, for the good reason that he came from Fiume and had a Slav name that was difficult to pronounce.

This was the time of the D'Annunzio campaign, and many refugees from Fiume had been given temporary homes by Lombard families, especially in Milan. I can still remember what an impression those women and old men and boys made on me when they walked through the Galleria [the arcade running between the Piazza del Duomo and the Piazza della Scala]. You could pick them out straight away, and people would hurry over to give them a kind word; but there were others who seemed to get fun out of making them feel embarrassed. I was still too young to understand, but I remember going home upset one day because I had seen a woman look rather contemptuously at a little group of those poor people and then say out loud "slaves"— a word which years later I came to know as the most appalling insult that can be leveled at our brothers who live under foreign domination. In our flat there wasn't even enough room for us, but my father wanted us to give a home to at least one refugee, and fate sent us that boy with the impossible name. Straight away we re-named him "Fiumano". There was only one Fiumano, but he was like ten boys put together. He might have been fifteen years old. He was fairly thickset, with big eyes that looked all the blacker under his bushy eye-brows. My mother took more care of him than of us. "I've got to be a mother to him as well," she used to say —and in that role she also gave him a few clouts. I must say that Fiumano deserved many more than he ever got because if we were scamps, he was much more of a menace. At worst we might smash a few street lamps with stones or frighten the whole block with our raids on the roof, but that was as far as we went. For Fi-umano such things were no more than a limbering up. The Fiume problem, D'Annunzio, and his Ronchi bri-gades—it all gave him a chance to show his real personality. And Fiumano was certainly one of the most likable madmen I've ever known.

Whenever my mother got to hear there was going to be a demonstration for or against D'Annunzio, she would rush to shut Fiumano in the house. But he always found some way to escape. So my mother would go out into the streets to look for him; we would tag along behind with a secret and boundless admiration for that boy who, all on his own, was capable of causing such turmoil. We used to find him in the most unimaginable and dangerous situations. Once, for instance, there was an anti-D'Annunzio demonstration, near the Arena. The police hadn't been able to scatter the demonstrators, and the *prefetto* had found it necessary to call in the army. The local army commander sent in a squadron of light cavalry who warned the demonstrators to disperse. The demonstrators took no notice, so the cavalry took up their positions, ready to charge.

Just at that moment, from out of a tangle of people beating hell out of one another, came Fiumano. His clothes were torn, his nose was bleeding, and he was madly yelling, "Long live Italian Fiume." In his wild enthusiasm he didn't see what was about to happen and, perhaps taking the cavalry for enemies, he moved boldly toward the squadron, which was just beginning to charge. My mother let out a shout. My heart was thumping furiously in my throat. A few yards away the cavalry, beautiful and terrible, were charging with drawn sabers, and people were dashing away in all directions. Fiumano must have finished up under the hooves of those charging beasts—perhaps he was already dead, certainly injured. But not at all. Less than a minute later Fiumano popped up next to us, in a frightening state but in fact unhurt, apart from his bloody nose, the result of a punch in the previous scuffle. What's more, he had come unscathed through a whole squadron of charging cavalry. This exploit, plus the blood stains, which were very decorative, enormously increased our childish admiration for Fiumano. And since my sister was the only girl in our family, he then made it his business to fall in love with her. My sister didn't share his feelings, but it can't be said that Fiumano, being such a spectacular tearaway, made no impression on her. "I'll go into the navy and become an admiral, then I'll come and collect you in my battleship," Fiumano declared. And it's not every day that a girl is offered the prospect of a fiancé waiting outside her house in a battleship—especially when she lives in Milan. Edda who had, and still has, a well-developed critical sense, told him that you couldn't come to Milan in a battleship—but for Fiumano that was a detail not worth bothering about.

"You can easily get to Milan through the canals from the Adriatic."

My sister listened wide-eyed. She thought a bit, then commented, "Fiumano's mad," and smiled.

That Fiumano was mad there was never any doubt in our house, especially if we recall how he disappeared out of our lives. From time to time Fiumano would go off into the streets to demonstrate for the unification of Fiume with Italy, and after a time we got used to it. But one day Fiumano disappeared—and all attempts to find him were in vain. My mother was terribly worried, thinking as always of her responsibility to another mother's son. My father, to tell the truth, was beginning to get fed up with him, all the more so as he had heard about the proposals of marriage the crazy lad had made to my sister. We searched for him a whole day and a whole night—in the streets, at the hospital, at the police station. Nothing. In the morning my father, looking for his slippers, noticed a big odd-looking bundle lying under his bed. It was Fiumano—sleeping peacefully. That was destined to be the last drop that made the cup of his patience overflow. The Fiume question was fortunately in the process of being peacefully solved, which freed my father from the last patriotic scruples. Fiumano packed his bags, swore to my sister that he would be back to get her in the battleship or even on foot, and left for good. Many years later a friend told me, by chance, that Fiumano was making his living playing the violin in the theater of a small town in Emilia—and that was the last I ever heard of him.

These were my sister's main "flirtations" before we moved from the Foro Buonaparte to the Via Mario Pagano, No. 39. It was a much smarter apartment, and it had the advantage—something which filled me and my brothers with pride—of an elevator. Edda was then sixteen; she was taking more care of her appearance, wore stockings, had got herself some smart dresses, and I noticed that she liked it when some older boy showed interest in her. Then, in 1928, it was decided to send her on a cruise to India. "A long trip will do her a lot of good," my father said. "It's time she became a young lady and got to know the world."

The decision was received at home with indescribable enthusiasm. For me and my brother Bruno, Edda's trip to India, the land of Tremal Naik and the Thugs, seemed a fantastic stroke of fortune—and we envied her. We had always admired Edda and now all the more so because she was going to the places so dear to our imagination. She was the best of us and it was right, after all, that she had been singled out by destiny. Edda embarked on the liner *Tevere* on December 10, 1928. The ticket cost 14,765 lire, a substantial sum in those days, and my father paid in the normal way, just like all the other cruise passengers, among whom were Senator Ettore Conti and his wife Gianna, who had arranged with my father to look after our sister. That year Edda spent Christmas in Ceylon, and we missed her very much. A few days later she sent us a letter saying that, while she was visiting the ruins at Anurhadapura, the ancient capital of the island, she had met a young Indian, very handsome, whose name was Sundaran.

Sundaran was a distinguished young man who had studied in England and was a friend of Gandhi's. He had gone to Anurhadapura from Benares specially to meet Mussolini's daughter and express the admiration of the Indian nationalists for the Duce, champion of oppressed peoples. The meeting made a great impression on Edda, coming as it did quite unexpectedly and so far from Italy; she wrote about it to my father and told him how proud she had felt to be his daughter. It was different for us boys: the idea of this Sundaran, suddenly appearing out of the ruins of a fabled city, had a Salgarian quality that was bound to push every other consideration into the background. We pictured him— tall, slim, with olive skin, big dark eyes and a turban, and with a long dagger (the handle studded with gems) stuck in his wide silk sash. "He'll be the right husband for Edda," said Bruno gravely. "She'll go over there with him and we can go and stay with her. We'll go tiger hunting."

All our plans foundered miserably when Edda came home. She was astonished when we questioned her so much about Sundaran's appearance, and she was very amused at our disappointment when she told us that Sundaran dressed more or less like a European, didn't even carry a penknife, and was studying to be a lawyer. Edda was already grown up: we were still children. The trip had widened the gulf between us to a point where it would be bridged only when we too had gone through the happy dreamy phase and emerged into real life. Edda's trip, as my father had foreseen, had done her good. She had become gentler and quieter, though some episodes had shown that deep down her nature was the same as ever—impetuous and uninhibited. Edda loved dancing, but she didn't hide her boredom at receptions, nor did she spare her sharp critical tongue when confronted by officials who wanted to ingratiate themselves with the Foreign Minister [Senator Conti] and heaped her with exaggerated courtesies as soon as they saw her. But in spite of several worrying "incidents," Edda learned a great deal and had improved substantially, thanks both to the intelligent advice she got from Signora Conti and to the environment in which she found herself. Like a well-bred girl she managed to curb the more tempestuous sides of her nature. She also paid attention to her appearance, which she had previously neglected, and stopped putting on too much lipstick. Furthermore, she had very quickly learned to make herself understood in English.

So on balance things had improved, and from then on my father and mother naturally began to think of the possibility of my sister taking a husband. It wasn't an easy matter. In every family, the choice of a likely husband for the daughter is always full of imponderables and worries, because the parents know from experience what a heavy responsibility they carry at this time. In Edda's case the question was more complicated, both because of her independent nature and because she didn't have any definite preferences—and also because what might have been all right from a strictly family and human point of view could have clashed with the political considerations my father had to take into account. Now that Edda had returned to Milan she had taken up a different way of life. She was more easygoing and more sure of herself, and she took an interest in lots of things that had previously meant little to her. She went out a lot, with boyfriends and girlfriends she had met on the cruise, she mixed with families from good Milanese society and, for a time, a young Jew. We boys saw him sometimes, and he made quite a hit with us. He was a good-looking young man, very pleasant and fond of sport, and we immediately liked him because he took an interest in what we said and made us feel we were on the same level, so that we were unaware of that wretched age difference. I remember hearing talk about that time of Edda taking quite a shine to him, but it was also said that there were many other considerations which made it inadvisable for their friendship to go on. Bruno and I, being small boys, weren't the slightest bit interested in this aspect, and when the grown-ups began discussing it we used to go the park to play. All I remember is that this likable young man disappeared from Edda's circle of friends.

Not long afterward I heard talk of another suitor, Count Pier Francesco Orsi Mangelli, a young gentleman from Romagna whose family my mother knew and with whom we remained very good friends, even though the marriage, which many considered a certainty, never came off. Many years later Pier Francesco and I served together in the same bomber squadron which was based, first at Ghedi, in the province of Brescia, and later at Grottaglie, near Taranto. I spent with him many intensely happy days, sometimes living through danger and sometimes having fun.

In the autumn of 1929 we moved to Rome and went to live in the Villa Torlonia. We were very sorry to leave Milan, not only because of the friends we had made there, but also because of the parochial idea that the real Italy finished at Florence—an idea which, as time went by and we took a more mature view of people and things, we radically revised. In fact it was in Rome, not long after we arrived there, that we heard talk of a new match for our sister. The young man in question, whom we had only gotten to know by name, was Galeazzo Ciano—and Bruno and I liked him immensely because of one very important factor: he was a diplomat and had been posted to Shanghai, a city where, we believed, the most fantastic adventures occurred every hour of the day and night. We had never seen him, and neither had Edda, and he had never seen my sister. Later we were to learn that Galeazzo Ciano's name had, by a process of elimination, emerged after a close look at all the circles where there might be a good chance of her meeting a future husband. I must say that I thought it unlikely that my sister, with her temperament, would fall in with such a solution and, above all, that she would be the happy wife she was with Galeazzo, in spite of all that has been said and written to the contrary.

Of course there was no lack of potential matches for my sister. Some people had even hoped for a marriage with Prince Umberto, and I'm bound to say this was the most senseless idea I heard put forward. Anyway, disregarding the heirs to the throne, there were plenty of men with royal connections who, in the opinion of some, could have been considered. My father, not to mention my mother, always discounted these suggestions. My father also rejected suggestions for a marriage with some representative of the Roman nobility. Such a marriage would have been in very poor taste, as everybody could have said that once the Mussolinis achieved power they tried to conceal their peasant origins (of which my father and all of us have always in truth been proud) behind an ancient coat of arms. So with the nobles, Roman or otherwise, discounted, there remained only one solution: to look among the new aristocracy of the armed forces and politics.

That was why, after mature reflection, my father's preference fell on the Ciano family. Costanzo Ciano was a supremely trusted friend, a man in whom my father had a blind faith and whom he greatly admired. Strong, hearty, genuine, and a legendary sea dog, old Ciano pleased my mother too; she recognized in him many of the good qualities of the common people. About Galeazzo, Costanzo's firstborn, we didn't know much. Before going into the diplomatic service, he had been in journalism, and he had also tried the theater—without much success. A play of his, staged by Bragaglia (like the work of many other young writers of the time, including Vergani and Campanile) had been a flop. Yet nobody questioned that Galeazzo was a talented young man. The worst that could be said of him was that he had taken some time to find his niche—and he seemed to have found it in the diplomatic service. His appearance was in contrast to his father's: very refined, always impeccable and well dressed, with a natural bent for high-society life and a personal manner that some people liked and many disliked, Galeazzo was to prove himself in every sense a man well suited to the life of a diplomat. He entered the service in 1927 and was posted to China, where he wasn't slow to give a good account of himself, and in Palazzo Chigi [the location in the Fascist era of the Italian Foreign Office] circles high hopes were entertained of him. It was while Galeazzo was in China that a whole set of circumstances developed which eventually led to his engagement to my sister.

In the summer of 1928 Edda went to Levanto to see Galeazzo's mother and sister, who had gone there for the bathing. Edda had never met Countess Ciano, but she immediately liked her. Edda's future mother-in-law, for her part, took an instant liking to my sister and, as always happens with mothers when they have a son far from home, the conversation came around to Galeazzo, his ways, his qualities, and his desire to make a successful career.

In spite of her rebellious streak, Edda had—and has —a strong feminine sensitivity. The kindly reception from Galeazzo's mother had made a great impression on her, and she was already keen to meet this young man who apparently had so many qualities. So Edda let her curiosity win the day and asked if she could see a photograph of him. Galeazzo's mother was surprised but deep down very pleased, and immediately opened her handbag in which, like all mothers, she carried a photographic memento of her precious son. Galeazzo was a really attractive man, with just the right amount of self-confidence to be interesting to an exceptional woman like Edda. I am convinced that from that day onward she began to take more seriously the idea of marrying Galeazzo Ciano.

This far she had been guided, though with the greatest delicacy, by our parents, but Edda knew that it was now up to her alone to decide. Neither my father nor my mother would have taken any further action, and least of all would they have forced her, if she herself had not wanted to marry this man. Nor was there any question of pressure being brought to bear by his parents, for all the fact that his mother had taken a liking to

Edda. His mother played no part in the matter, and as for his father, it was not surprising that he had considerable doubts to overcome before giving his consent to the marriage: with his proud upstanding character he didn't want to give the impression of seeking to link up with a powerful man through his daughter's marriage, even though the Duce was his friend.

And so Edda was, strange as it may seem, absolutely free to make up her own mind. From that day spent with Galeazzo's mother, up to the engagement and then the marriage, it was obvious that Edda had made her choice knowingly and with passionate conviction. Time was to show that she had made a good choice.

VII

Somebody else who had been present at the conversation between Edda and her future mother-in-law on the beach at Levanto was Maria, Galeazzo's sister—and she played an important part in paving the way for the first meeting between Edda and my future brother-in-law. Maria was a pleasant, capable girl, at once shy and determined, polite and prickly. But she was ruled by an absurd and—as it was later to prove—fatal obsession about putting on weight. She was as thin as a rake, and she only kept herself alive by nibbling bread and an occasional olive, refusing to eat anything more substantial. Costanzo Ciano was in despair; his approach to life and good eating was that of a healthy, jolly old sailor—and one from Livorno at that. He adored his family, and in particular this girl who, he felt instinctively, had special need of his attention; but he didn't know how he could remedy the situation, except by asserting his authority from time to time. Maria didn't dare oppose him openly, so she would sit at table and pretend to eat. But she would choose her moment and, with the skill of a conjuror, put her napkin up in front of her mouth and let the food drop under the table.

Sometimes, as if this weren't enough, she would go to her room, where she kept a bottle of vinegar hidden, and drink several small glassfuls. We boys liked Maria a lot. Edda was fond of her and she of Edda, possibly because they had such different temperaments: whereas Edda was sociable, dynamic, aggressive, Maria was reserved and unable to face reality with assurance. Proof of this, and alas painful proof, was to come from her marriage to Count Magistrati. The wedding was nearly called off at the last minute because of the emotional state the poor girl got herself into a few hours before the ceremony, with the result that she had to go to bed in a high fever, and her parents—and the distressed bridegroom—had to perform miracles of gentle persuasion before she would get dressed and come to the church where my father, who was one of the witnesses, was waiting with many others.

Then Maria, with one of those bursts of initiative characteristic of shy people, decided to take my sister under her wing and arrange for Edda to meet her brother, in the most favorable circumstances possible. The meeting took place at the end of 1929, when Galeazzo was transferred from China to the Italian Embassy at the Holy See. From what I remember, Edda and Galeazzo first set eyes on each other at the Teatro Reale dell'Opera, in Rome, during a performance of *The Barber of Seville*. In the interval between the second and third acts, Edda went to the Cianos' box to say hello to Maria and to the Countess who, I believe, received her with special enthusiasm, knowing that Galeazzo was there. They barely had time to exchange a few words, because just at that moment my father, unwittingly spoiling the two girls' plans, called Galeazzo over to his box for a talk on the latest political and military developments in China. I don't know whether Edda and Galeazzo met again after the opera. Bruno and I no longer took much notice of Edda's doings, as she was already a young woman, and we didn't have the same interests any more. Yet we sensed there was something in the air: Edda was going out more than usual, at home she was more cheerful, and she listened to records for hours on end—in a word, she was showing all the symptoms of a girl in love.

At that time—it was 1930—our family was at last enjoying a period of calm and relative prosperity. After 1925–26, which were the last years of upheaval in internal Italian politics, a solution had been found to the one remaining problem left over from the Risorgimento—the relations between Church and State. With honorable agreement reached in the Concordat, a peaceful period opened which brought a resurgence of our national life in all its sectors and also the greatest and most lasting achievements of the Fascist regime. Italian prestige was growing all the time. The rest of the world watched Italy with friendly admiration in the effort she was making, with such scanty resources, to pull herself out of the postwar chaos and re-establish her place in the world. This was the period of the first invasions of package tourists. Millions of foreigners, especially Anglo-Saxons (with baggy shorts, checked jackets, big caps, pipes, their wives with thick stockings and stiff gray skirts), were beginning to discover an Italy they had never read about in their books. Rome was the main attraction both for tourists and for pilgrims who, after the Lateran Treaties, came more and more often and in ever greater numbers—the high point being reached with the celebrations for Holy Year (there were further special celebrations in 1931). To Rome also came personalities from the fields of culture, the arts, sports, and politics, from Italy and many other countries; and the room at the Palazzo Venezia [the Prime Minister's office, the equivalent of England's No. 10 Downing Street], where they waited to be received by my father, was a daily barometer of Rome's attraction. There were musicians such as Mascagni, Puccini, Paderewski, Respighi, and Alfano; scientists such as Marconi, Fermi, Aston, Beher, Compton, Millikan, Perrin, and Richardson (the scientists had come to Rome for the first world congress of nuclear physics, and their names were destined to figure many times in the history of science); writers such as Gemito and Pirandello; politicians such as Churchill, Chamberlain, Dolfuss, Litvinoff, Laval, and Cardinal Pacelli (later to become Pope); men of the theater such as Gordon Craig; and sportsmen such as Carnera. All audiences were given at the Palazzo Venezia, with the single exception made for Gandhi, who was received at the Villa Torlonia with his inseparable goat. We boys peeped through the shutters while my father was talking in the garden with the small austere man who carried such an aura of moral dignity. When he had left, my father came back into the house and found us laughing, in our blissful ignorance, about the goat. He looked at us sternly. The meeting had moved him, and that great figure's extreme simplicity of manner had confirmed my father's esteem for him. "That man and his goat," he said, "are shaking the British Empire." And he left us wondering how it was possible to play such a major role in history without using armies, navies, and airplanes.

In that confident and hopeful atmosphere, the Villa Torlonia was a peaceful home for us all. Sometimes the Cianos, husband and wife, came to see us. I don't think they had yet said anything about Edda and Galeazzo to my parents, but all four of them knew, without having to make unnecessary speeches about it, that the two young people would soon be confirming their now obvious desire to get married. Carolina Ciano inspired a certain awe in me and Bruno. She was a good-looking woman, tall and slim, with a gentle, noble bearing—altogether too much for us. Costanzo Ciano, on the other hand, was vigorous, hearty, and very lively; he was the very incarnation of the sea dogs we had imagined and admired in our adventure stories. What's more, it turned out that he had had quite a few adventures, and real ones. Even my father, who was normally very reserved with his colleagues, including those who were closest to him, opened up and was unusually forthcoming with Costanzo. It was obvious that he felt perfectly at ease with him and didn't need to weigh his words, knowing full well what firm, warm-hearted loyalty he could count on from Costanzo—I should say, from Costanzone [old Costanzo], which is what we called him as a sign of special esteem; and this name, which amused him very much, came into general use and was adopted, as time went on, by Edda's children.

One evening Bruno and I came home from the cinema—it would have been about eight o'clock—to find all the servants scurrying about. People were coming to dinner. We were surprised, because my parents never entertained people to meals at the Villa Torlonia, and the only outsiders who occasionally ate with us were certain schoolfriends of Bruno's and mine. We went to my mother who, with that aversion she had for any kind of smart worldly occasion—something which, to tell the truth, has more than once been the cause of misunderstandings and unnecessary embarrassment— told us that the Cianos were coming to dinner.

"All of them," she added, desperately worried about the number (three, in fact), which to her seemed exceptional. But she quickly pulled herself together and ordered us to go and put on our best clothes—short blue trousers, blue jacket, and white shirt with the collar open outside the jacket. We were hungry and annoyed about this unforeseen development. We ran to the stairs and, having checked that we had put enough distance between ourselves and our mother, gave vent to our feelings with an "Egh, what a bore" and then ran for it: in those days my mother was still extraordinarily quick when she wanted to give us a cuff.

"All" the Cianos—Costanzo, Carolina, and Galeazzo —arrived at about nine o'clock. We sat down at once to eat. The meal was a very simple one (in our house there were never high-class cooks or servants—just good Romagnola girls always chosen by my mother), and the atmosphere was very cordial, thanks especially to my father and Costanzone, who were in a class by themselves when their good humor was in full spate. Bruno and I looked on all this with a certain detachment. There had been more than enough pointers as to where things were leading, including this formal dinner, which was unusual in our house. My sister hardly glanced at us boys, and neither did the others—obviously they were interested only in what they were talking about. So as soon as the fruit course was over we looked across to my mother for permission to leave the table: she nodded, and we left them sitting there.

A few days later preparations began for a really big reception—the first and last to be given at the Villa Torlonia. For my mother it was, I think, one of the greatest trials of her life. In an attempt to get herself organized, since it was impossible not to have the reception, my mother had asked my father to make her a list of all the guests. It's well known that men are hopeless at this sort of thing, but my father had a secretary and a staff to handle social events, so he passed on to them the unwelcome task. It was decided to invite only a few intimate friends, and my mother was given a list of about thirty people—an awe-inspiring number for her, but one she determined to face with courage. Of course the number didn't stay at thirty. My father would phone to say we should also invite so-and-so, because otherwise that person would take offense. Then my father's secretary would suggest including somebody else, or otherwise it would look very bad. Then it was Costanzone saying he was very sorry, but we would have to include so-and-so and somebody else too. The thirty people became forty, then fifty, then ninety. Two days later, on April 23, 1930, in the gardens of the Villa Torlonia, the "few intimate friends" had grown to five hundred and twelve and my mother had, several hours before, given up protesting. My father, who at first had been cross with her and later amused by her furious outbursts, appreciated the human and genuine way she felt; he understood her instinctive dislike of any sort of official gathering, and of all those who belonged to a different social class. So he found the right words to show his sympathy, and my mother repaid him by receiving all the guests with miraculous sweetness and courtesy.

The newspapers of the day described the reception in a way that would have given enormous pleasure to any lady of the house, always granted she wasn't "Donna Rachele." Because my mother, having done her duty, took absolutely no interest in what the society columns had to say. The reception was attended by forty-seven excellencies with their respective wives, all with the title of "Donna." Also among the guests were ambassadors, ministers accredited to the Quirinal,* and many of the finest names from the Italian aristocracy—the ducal family of the Sforzas, the Marchese and Marchesa

*The Quirinal Palace was the city residence of the kings of Italy, so "the Quirinal" denoted the Italian monarchy and civil government—as opposed to the Vatican authorities.

De Vulci, Count and Countess Gaddi Pepoli, Prince and Princess Vannutelli, Baron and Baroness Blanc, Count and Countess Macchi De Cellere, Prince and Princess Chigi Albani, the Marchese and Marchesa Misciatelli; there were also senators, deputies, bosses of the big newspapers, and the leading Party officials. The betrothed couple were at a table next to one where sat my father and mother, Carolina and Maria Ciano, and Monsignor Borgoncini Duca. My sister, so the newspapers said, wore a printed pink chiffon dress, but Bruno and I didn't even notice because we were very busy going around the assembled throng of guests, having great fun looking at all the gentlemen in their top hats (it was an open-air reception) and the ladies in those horrible little *cloche* hats and soft fluffy furs with only their faces, white with powder, peeping out. "They look like characters out of a Ridolini [a comedian of the day whose English name was Larry Semon] film," Bruno whispered to me, giving me a dig with his elbow, when we passed some particularly imposing gentleman or highly painted dame. We tried to be cheerful, but we weren't really. Like everybody else in our family, we have never shown our feelings to the outside world. I've heard members of our family comment on births and deaths, good fortune and disasters, with a simple "Oh"—because that's our temperament. Which doesn't mean we feel things any the less: on the contrary. That day Bruno and I felt that Edda was lost to us. She belonged now to another world, she could no longer lead our expeditions on the roofs and in the woods. And, worse still, we too were moving in our turn, and without her, into another phase of our lives.

All this was too complicated for us to understand clearly: it just left us with a numbed feeling which, after a time, gave way to depression. "Look at him," Bruno said, indicating Galeazzo. He looked fine in his tails, our brother-in-law. He was a good-looking young man, full of attentions and smiles for our sister. But he wasn't the type we had imagined and felt entitled to expect, because a man who had been to Shanghai shouldn't have been like that—so polite, so elegant, and so unlike a Salgari hero. Bruno looked up at the very tall pines around the Villa Torlonia. The sun was almost setting and the trunks on one side of the garden were glowing red like embers. The Quartetto della Filarmonica Chigiana was playing classical music in honor of Edda and Galeazzo. "You know," Bruno went on, casting an expert eye over the pines, "Galeazzo couldn't even climb a fig tree." He shook his head and waited for me to disapprove. "I don't think he could either," I said, "but if Edda's happy . . ."

The next day, a Thursday, there could be no more doubt about her happiness: the priest of the church of San Giuseppe, Don Giovenale Pascucci, asked her the question. She said yes, and became Countess Ciano.

The last few hours before a wedding are always, in any family, full of indescribable bustle and excitement, but in our house we reached the supreme heights of confusion because of what my mother added to the already difficult circumstances. I shall always remember it: only a few minutes before the ceremony was due to begin, she had still hardly begun changing and was going around the house trying to do a thousand things at once, with the result that she couldn't do anything and, moreover, got in the way of my father, who was now ready in his tails and white gloves and was frantically searching for his opera hat—which Bruno and I had got hold of because we loved opening and closing it like accordion players. In all this chaos Edda retained, like a goddess, our family's highest qualities of coolness and her usual sense of humor. She wore a white dress by Montorsi in magnificent satin specially woven in Como, and flowing lace, a gift from the Senate, which was gathered into a garland of pearls and orange blossom. Two little pages, nervous and excited, waited to carry the enormously long train. It was obvious that their mothers had been preparing them for that moment through days and days of rigorous training, and they were terrified of making a mistake—which in fact they promptly did.

Edda came into the church on her father's arm, under an arch of drawn swords held by the Duce's Musketeers. Behind her came Galeazzo with Countess Ciano, Costanzo and my mother, and the witnesses— Dino Grandi [the man who in 1943, in the Fascist Grand Council, put the motion that led to the arrest and imprisonment of Mussolini], my uncle Arnaldo, De Vecchi di Val Cismon, and Prince Torlonia. The little cortege was met by the priest who accompanied the bridal pair to the prie-dieu, while the two families took their places on either side of the altar. The church was a mass of flowers. "It was as if," wrote the reporter from the

Corriere della Sera, "all the gardens of Rome had denuded themselves to send their roses and azaleas and lilies and lilac to the Duce's daughter."

My mother later sent all the flowers to the cemetery of the Campo Verano, to be laid on the crypt dedicated to those fallen in war.

People were thronging the Via Nomentana. The luckier ones even knew what was on the list of wedding gifts: the Pope had sent a rosary of gold and malachite, the King and Queen a gold bracelet with precious stones, the Chamber of Deputies a valuable tea service, the Senate the Burano lace, the PNF [the National Fascist Party] a magnificent brooch, and the Governor of Rome a ruby bracelet; while from all the cities and provinces and Fascist Federations, and from countless private citizens (I can say this today with no fear of being called a mouthpiece for the Ministry of Popular Culture, the official propaganda department) had come a great variety of presents accompanied by the most affectionate messages, very often anonymous, which showed that my father was really loved by the people.

After the ceremony, when the couple was on the way to Naples and thence to Capri, a relative calm finally settled on our house. The rooms were like a battlefield, my mother had a terrible headache, and my father and Galeazzo's parents were in an emotional state. Galeazzo's parents came to dinner with us. At first neither they nor my parents talked much. They couldn't help it, but they were all thinking of the two young people who had gone away, and the meal threatened to end rather sadly. But soon my father and Costanzone began recalling the day's events and accidents, describing the guests' expressions and what they had worn, and morale rose sharply.

But when Bruno and I went up to bed and took off our best clothes, we felt a bit depressed because they were all we had left from that terribly important day. "And she was the one," grumbled Bruno, "who was always saying she couldn't stand Tuscans."

Which was true. My sister—and one would have to ask her why this was—had always said, ever since she was a little girl, that she would never marry either a Tuscan or a lawyer, and of course she married Galeazzo, who came from Livorno and had a degree in law.

"They'll certainly be happy," I said stiffly, repeating the words I had heard an old lady say and which I had liked very much. Indeed Edda and Galeazzo were, especially in those first years, truly happy. After the honeymoon at Capri, they left for China, where Galeazzo had been appointed Consul General. My sister always recalls that period of her life with great joy. In Shanghai and then in Peking, from 1930 to 1933, she found what she had been looking for: a busy, enjoyable, varied life in a completely different world, on which she could stamp her strong personality at will, as if it were one enormous toy. Beside her she had a young man who was pleased with himself, with his career, and with a wife who in a very short time had won admiration and popularity everywhere in that difficult world.

Early in 1931, when the first disorders occurred in Shanghai and many foreigners took fright and fled,

Edda was the city's first lady. The smart set meekly followed her tastes in clothes and entertainment and sport, forgetting that they were copying a woman who had been brought up not in expensive colleges, but in poverty and the cruel vicissitudes of political battle.

The local English-language paper, seeking to stop the exodus of foreigners, used only one weapon. It published a full-page picture of Edda, with the caption: "Shanghai's first lady won't leave."

It was in Shanghai that, on October 1, 1931, Edda's first child, Fabrizio, was born. Why they gave him that name, I don't know. Nobody at home was called that, and we all thought it was a bit affected because the child had also been given the names of Benito and Costanzo. My mother, in particular, disliked the name Fabrizio, but it would be useless to look for a rational explanation. I believe my mother's disapproval of that name which, in fact, was no more pretentious than the other two names, was only an expression of a deeper-rooted complex—her constant uneasiness. My mother has always remained a woman of simple tastes, and it's no secret that being the Duce's wife never went to her head. In her age-old common sense, she has never trusted success and power, and so she had her doubts about her daughter's marriage. Perhaps she would have liked a young working-class man, somebody ordinary, not mixed up in politics, and certainly not in international high society. My mother has always been attracted and at the same time repelled by that world, and she has shown it—hiding under the most sweeping contempt her vague fear of being judged by it. So this explains why Galeazzo, who by temperament was perfectly cut out for a way of life that was alien to my mother, and whose career, anyway, was accentuating his rarefied way of life, could not be completely to her liking.

But I would like to say that this did not in any way stem, as has often been written and said, and as even Edda has sometimes complained, from a direct and personal antipathy. In fact, on several occasions my mother took Galeazzo's part against her daughter. It was something quite different, going much further back, even back, I believe, to the ancient and humiliating distinction between the *signori* and the poor—which progress has not erased even today. My mother wasn't on that side of the *signori;* and perhaps unwittingly, she prejudged everything emanating from that side of the divide. Galeazzo was on that other side. And he had taken Edda over there. Nothing wrong in that, of course, and, what is more, it was the life that Edda enjoyed, and Galeazzo was the perfect husband for her. But my mother, perhaps, never understood that. Which is why both she and Edda, and indirectly my father, suffered more than they need have done.

VIII

That afternoon of April 28, 1945, it was so cold it seemed like winter, in the sick-room of the Gallio College in Como. Or perhaps it was just that I felt cold, because the nervous tension of those last terrible days of our adventure was too much. Since arriving at the College the previous evening, I hadn't managed a wink of sleep.

I was sure that any moment somebody would come and shoot me, just because I was Mussolini's son. It's difficult to say what one feels at such moments. I had already faced death several times in the war—had faced it, what's more, in the air, without the ultimate solace of the ground under my feet and the protective feeling it gives, even if that's illusory. But in the war it had been different. I have heard talk of men "who are never afraid," but I don't believe they exist. All men are afraid: it's just that some manage to do their duty in spite of it, and others don't. In the war it had been possible to do one's duty because of the thought that one was fighting for one's country and, if the end came, one would be leaving behind a name that would be honored and remembered. But there wasn't that compensation any more, there was only fear left, that boundless, cold, useless fear of dying without much hope of resisting with arms or words. And in my case, it would not be dying at the hands of a foreigner, but at the hands of men born in my own country, men who would insult me in my own language and—which was worse—would think of me as a real enemy.

These were my thoughts as I looked at the row of iron sick-room beds of dull, chipped white enamel. They were all empty. Many a time I had longed for a clean bed and a couple of hours of peace as the ultimate luxury. Now, in all that silence, and with all the need I had for rest, I could hardly lie down. With me, probably immersed in the same thoughts, were Orio Ruberti and Vanni Teodorani [the author's cousin], not just relations but, above all, faithful friends.

We had brought with us a little Phonola radio, and we kept it on only very quietly, as we had been advised to do by the Somaschi fathers when they took us in, so that we could hear what the "others" were saying— those who had won. Suddenly—it would have been about five o'clock—the partisan hymn was interrupted and we heard the excited voice of an announcer say: "Attention, attention." A few seconds passed, and then another voice, triumphant, told us that "justice had been done." Mussolini "and all the other Fascists who were with him" had been shot.

I, like many other people, had foreseen it would end like this. I had argued that we should stay in Milan, barricaded in the Prefecture, and hold out until the arrival of the Anglo-Americans. It was my father who had wanted to go to Como and once there, having heard the news (which had been deliberately leaked) that the Allies would raze the town to the ground if it harbored the last pocket of Fascist resistance, he decided to move on again, toward Dongo.

It was a shattering blow. We were silent for a long time, incapable of gathering our thoughts, incapable of reacting, numbed by the slaughter that was now on the rampage. My first thought was for my mother. I was certain she had found refuge in Switzerland with Romano and Anna Maria, as had been planned: I didn't know then that the Swiss frontier authorities at Ponte Chiasso, having asked for instructions from their Government, had refused to let my mother and brother and sister in—a unique lapse, I believe, and an ungrateful one, in the story of traditional Swiss hospitality. I was to learn later that my mother, for all the unknown dangers of staying in Italy, and all the agonizing worry about the fate of my father, whose death she had not yet heard about, was almost relieved to receive that blank refusal, because at least she would not have to accept hospitality like some humiliating charity.

So (without dwelling on this any further) my mother, Romano, and Anna Maria went back to Como and, after trying unsuccessfully to get on the road and rejoin my father's column, they found refuge in the house of a Fascist, where they were at last able to rest, after spending three nights practically without sleep. When they woke up again, the manhunt had already begun. Motionless behind the shutters, my mother and brother and sister saw a young man running away in his pajamas from a nearby hospital. Within seconds they saw him caught, surrounded, and killed. That horrible spectacle persuaded my mother, concerned to save my brother and sister at all costs, to destroy the papers she had on her which would have immediately revealed her identity. So she hastily burned in a little cast-iron stove the manuscripts of *Parlo con Bruno** and *Storia di un anno,*** several letters written by Rommel and Kesselring to my father during the last phases of the war, documents referring to the period 1939–40 and to July 25, 1943, and finally—something which was immensely painful to my mother—the last letter my father wrote to her, the previous night, in the knowledge that the end was near. In fact, it was a precaution she need never have taken because, in the afternoon of April 29, a "people's *commissario"* came to the house and took my mother and brother and sister to the police station, and

---

*The book Mussolini wrote soon after the death of his son Bruno on August 7, 1941. Bruno was killed when he crashed in a prototype four-engine warplane which he was piloting. Proceeds of the book went to the orphans of Italian airmen killed in the war.

**First published anonymously as a series in the Italian daily, *Corriere della Sera*. The thirty articles, which described events between October 1942 and September 1943, were published under the title *Storia di un anno (Story of a Year)*. But anonymity could not be maintained because the whole of Italy soon recognized Mussolini's highly individual style. The articles were published in a volume under the title *Il bastone e la carota (The Stick and the Carrot)*, a phrase Churchill is said to have used about the Italian people.

from there to the San Donnino Prison, where they were put in separate cells. I would rather, for my country's sake, pass over what happened in that prison, where no horror or terror was spared my poor mother and her children, until, fortunately, they were handed over to the American Command and at least had the certainty of staying alive.

So far as I knew, as I waited in an agony of impotent grief and anxiety at the sick-room window, only Edda had that certainty. She was in Switzerland with her children, she could go out into the streets, go into a shop, stop and talk with people at a café—and once again all this seemed impossible, because Switzerland was over there, a few minutes' walk away, as it had been that night when I stood in the darkness and saw the glittering lights of Ponte Chiasso. I could have had everything over there, a few minutes' walk away—my mother, my sisters, my brother. And my father had been here a few hours before. I had some time previously moved my wife and children from Gargnano to a house in the outskirts of Como. I was fairly easy in my mind about my own family: I knew I could count on my wife, a woman outwardly frail but capable of showing resourcefulness and pluck in moments of danger. And Gina, Bruno's widow, was in Como with her daughter Marina. But I had no news of any of them, and neither could I get any. The radio went on pouring out speeches, news flashes, partisan hymns. It was all finished—except for us. We were all that was left— waiting till that voice came on the radio again, "Attention, attention," to say that another of us had been shot.

With my two companions I lived through several
months of strange imprisonment in the Gallio College.
The school year was over, the students had gone home,
and we were moved from the sick-room to the boys'
empty dormitories. We were advised not to go out under any circumstances whatever. During those months
we came to realize that man has unsuspected powers of
adaptation and resistance. Together we made up our
minds not to give in to anxiety and discomfort, but to
fight and keep ourselves in good shape and ready for
anything. Apart from the radio we had nothing with
which to fill the endless hours. But we had devised a
program which, together with the two important
events of the day—the frugal meals brought to us by
Brother Guglielmo—included conversation, rest, and
physical exercises. We would walk one behind the
other around the beds, having first carefully measured
out a course, till we had done a certain number of
kilometers, essential to any recluse's health.

Brother Guglielmo was a young Piedmontese of
medium stature, with a crew cut and a kindly smile. He
used to bring us the college food and stay about half an
hour to talk. Every day we worked out possible courses
of action and made plans. Hope, somebody has said, is
a disease against which none of us has any defense—
which is true. It certainly applied to us three, because
the fact that so far they hadn't come to get us seemed
as time went on to confirm our right to live; after taking
it for granted, in the early days, that we would be shot,
we began to think in terms of a thirty-year prison term,
which in those circumstances seemed the greatest good

fortune we could hope for, although we knew we had not done anything wrong.

Having crossed the frontier (and one needs to have lived this experience to know what it means) between death and life, albeit in prison, optimism began to bubble up in our plans. We decided to make contact with the American Command in Milan, and we told them we were in the Gallio College. The Americans, using the same trusted intermediary as we had used to get in touch with them, told us they would come and fetch us as soon as possible. This undertaking (and I don't know why it was never kept) reassured us, especially as there were numerous signs that somebody had talked and that our presence in the college was no longer a secret —something which, moreover, worried the Somaschi fathers, who feared that sooner or later they would be in trouble on our account.

A false alarm caused by the arrival of a number of partisans at the College—we all thought they had come to get us, whereas that wasn't their intention—made us act fast. We decided to leave and split up, so that we wouldn't be too conspicuous. By good luck we made contact with several old friends and, with the help of my little store of petrol, which I had personally buried near the house where my wife and children were hiding, we prepared to set off. Vanni said he wanted to go to Rome, while Orio, after many adventures, was to land in Rapallo. Although every plan we had made went wrong at the last moment because of some tiny and seemingly unimportant detail, I also found myself in Rapallo, where I took refuge in an orphanage. Not long afterwards my family came to Rapallo and stayed in a small inconspicuous villa. I spent the whole of the autumn and part of the winter in the orphanage, in a small room where I could hear the chatter of small children in their classrooms.

It's difficult to describe the squalor and privations of those days in the orphanage, and yet I am always moved afresh when I think of them, because the poor nuns, who denied themselves everything just to keep their little orphans from going hungry, showed me how to live and be happy in humility and silence.

A whole world had collapsed, and I too felt how poor and precarious my existence was, as I was forced to hide first in one place, then another. Yet it was borne in on me that life begins again each morning and can always be ennobled if we think less of ourselves and more of others. I used to get my wife to bring me sheets of cardboard—some evenings she would come to meet me in the dark near the orphanage—and I would make little cars and lorries, which the nuns used to give to the children. I became very skillful and learned to make the precious cardboard go a long way. The nuns told me that the children were pleased—which did me an infinite power of good. But this too was to be only an interlude, because one day I was warned that the partisans knew where I was hiding and would be coming to get me. There was no time to lose: I had to be on the move again. Brother Guglielmo managed, I don't know how, to get hold of two bicycles; and during the night, after panting up those fierce hills, we rode into Genoa. There I was picked up by a friend from Rome who, through some amazing fiddling, had concocted an odd-looking pass for his car. It was a rectangular piece of paper on which figured a big red star and a mass of scribbled illegible signatures which he had then plastered with equally illegible rubber stamps. I laughed when I saw it, and told him I was sure that a car with a pass like that would be stopped by the police inside two kilometers. But there was little choice. So we climbed into the car, which my friend had decided belonged to the Russian Embassy, and set off for Rome. Contrary to my predictions, we got to Rapallo, where I was able to say hello to my wife and children, and then proceeded quietly on our way. Every now and then we were stopped by the police or Allied roadblocks, but my friend's pass worked every time. At Livorno two gigantic American military policemen drew themselves up stiffly to attention as we passed unhindered—from which I concluded that wars and revolutions are undoubtedly tragedies but with many a touch of farce.

In Rome I found hospitality at a college run by a likable French priest. I had grown a beard, and the priest often let me go down to meals when he had guests, so that I could get an idea of the way feelings were running in the country; but he always made me, for safety's sake, put on an anonymous-looking black cassock.

In the meantime my wife was bringing off an exploit straight out of a novel. She had made contact with an undercover international organization which, on payment of a large sum of money, would obtain a false passport. When she told me about her plan, I laughed

—just as I had laughed about my friend's car and the Russian pass he had concocted. And yet an Argentinian passport arrived, complete with stamps and signatures, and the most pernickety bureaucrat could not have asked for better.

In it was a photograph of me with beard, mustache, and glasses. I figured as a citizen of Argentina, fully entitled, moreover, to return to "his" country. I remember that when my wife brought me the passport, I was just speechless. But from that moment on I began changing many of my ideas about women's capabilities.

So, leaving for Argentina became the thought uppermost in my mind, but at the same time I wanted to see the other members of the family at least once again. The events of the immediate postwar period had scattered us and kept us apart for a long time.

My mother, Anna Maria, and Romano, after being handed over to the Americans, who were very cordial, had been passed to the British, who were much more severe and sent them to the concentration camp at Terni. There my mother and brother and sister lived at first in strict isolation which was later relaxed, so that they were able to mix with a few other prisoners. My mother, with that surprising vitality of hers, had begun reorganizing her life and that of her children, beginning all over again from scratch, with the help of only a broom and a piece of soap—which for her have always been basic to any form of civilized living. After a few months the British Command transferred my mother and her children from Terni to the island of Forio d'Ischia. There living conditions, though extremely poor, were better because of the warmth and kindness of the local people. But soon new troubles came along. My mother fell gravely ill, and so did Romano; Anna Maria was due to undergo an operation, and there wasn't the money to pay for it. Once again, though, my mother with her exceptional courage was to rise to the occasion, and she finally got permission to return to Rome.

Just then I heard of another surprise development. My sister Edda had at the end of the war come back to Italy from Switzerland, to see what she could do for the other members of the family. She thought she had nothing to fear, but in fact she was arrested, separated from her children (who had been left in the care of Carolina Ciano), and confined on the island of Lipari. But she too got permission to return to the mainland, so I was able to see her again.

Gina, alas, had not been able to stay with us any longer. The partisans had been to search her house, and had found only a copy of *Il bastone e la carota (The Stick and the Carrot)*.* A furious woman partisan, wearing trousers and carrying a machine gun, hurled the book at Gina's little daughter Marina (who was then five years old) and bruised her on the temple. They completely shaved Gina's mother's hair, but in the end they went away, and all danger with them. Yet fate had decided that little Marina was to lose not only her father but also her mother, for Gina was drowned in the most tragic yet banal way while going by motorboat to

*See page 123.

the wedding reception of a woman friend on the other side of Lake Como. An unexpectedly big wave overturned the boat: Gina, who was a poor swimmer, was trapped under the boat and drowned before the others could save her.

So it was that for the first time for nearly three years (a relatively short time, but it seemed very long to me because of all we had been through) we all met again. We had chosen Pompeii as the most easily accessible spot from the various places we were coming from. It was an autumn day, but still soft and clear. We sat on the grass—my mother, Romano, Anna Maria, Edda, and myself. As usual, none of us showed how deeply moved we were. We looked at one another and chatted, as if everything was normal, as if we had seen one another only a few days before—and as if my father, Bruno, Galeazzo, and Gina hadn't died. My mother opened a big bag and pulled out some food wrapped in greaseproof paper—she was just the same as ever, looking after us with the same thoughtfulness. Ever since 1933, more or less, each of us had gone his own way: from being children we had grown up, had our own families, fought in the war, and had our different adventures, which we had had to live through without even the comfort of facing danger together—except for me and Bruno, for we had been inseparable till his death.

And yet all this—and I realized it that day—had brought us even closer together. I would leave for Argentina knowing that our family was a close-knit spiritual force and that none of us would ever be alone again. I looked at Edda, my generous and independent sister, in a new light. Now she had come back to be with my mother: they were slowly passing each other slices of bread and fruit, and finding the strength to smile. It was all over, all past, and a new life was beginning for the Mussolini family. My mother and sister had fought so desperately for their husbands—and lost them: but they themselves had survived, and they were strong and ready to fight again.

I sensed that from now on they would fight together and would never leave each other again. In this joyful knowledge I said good-bye to these dear ones and prepared for my departure. On December 4, 1946, I made my way from Rome to Genoa, where I went to the quayside to board the *Philippa*, an old ship flying the Panamanian flag.

Even today, when I find myself at a frontier and the police ask me for documents (and today I have my proper passport, I've shaved off the beard, and I wear glasses not for disguise but because I no longer see so well as I used to), I feel a vague sense of alarm. I certainly felt it that day in Genoa, when the passenger in front of me moved through the barrier and the official put out his hand to take my passport, the one on which I figured as a citizen of Argentina. All officials at frontier posts look carefully at passports, and I think they sometimes give themselves important airs. But for me, at that moment, every glance, every hesitation, meant only suspicion.

Here we go, I thought—he's going to say my passport isn't in order. He's seen through my little game and he's going to stop me. I can't leave. I've had it.

How long that torment lasted, I don't know. It seemed endless, but it was probably only a few minutes. Then I heard him say, "O.K., straight ahead," and I had the presence of mind to pretend not to understand, as if I were expecting him to say it in Spanish—*Pase adelante.* I crossed the quay, reached the gangway, and stepped on board. Only then, when I was leaning over the rails and watching my wife, standing down there with our children, did I know that I was safe; and I smiled, even though my wife, who up till then had remained composed, began crying. The voyage was uneventful. I was traveling second-class (I couldn't afford first-class with money so short), but after a few days at sea I found myself spending a lot of time in the first-class section, in company with Varzi, Villoresi, and Canestrini, who, with a team of mechanics, were going to South America for a series of motor races. They recognized me immediately, in spite of my beard and glasses, and invited me to join in endless games of poker. But they had the tact not to say anything, not even to me. The voyage lasted twenty-two days, and not once was I called by my own name (except by a young Communist who was my cabin mate); not once did I have to say anything about myself or our family or the war. We talked about everything—except those subjects. And I must say that especially then, when things were so difficult, I felt immensely grateful to those men who with such tact and quick wit were able to put me immediately and completely at my ease.

The rest of my time in Argentina isn't part of this story. As soon as I landed I looked for a job. I worked for a few months, still under my false name—till one day I judged the time was ripe, and I presented myself to the Chief of Police, General Velasco, and told him everything. He was very human and understanding, and I obtained a normal resident's permit. Soon after that the Italian Consulate gave me back my own passport, the one with which I returned to Italy.

So I was settled, with only the problems that face anybody who emigrates to a foreign country and has to live on what he can earn. My life had taken a different direction—one which still persists today. Soon I was joined by my family, I got a house, small but comfortable, and a fairly secure job. I was tolerably well off. But there was a deep sadness still. During those years, while I was so far from Italy, my mother and sister were fighting, without me, to save the last piece of property that was truly ours but had still been sternly denied us: my father's remains.

That's another story—and a long one. It went on for twelve years, during which two women, Edda and my mother, knocked on every door to get what is not denied even to the wives and daughters of criminals. The hatred that drove many to trample on the graves of those who had fallen fighting on the other side of the barricades (as if political passions should not cease with death) had been placated, and all over Italy cemeteries began to appear where fallen Fascists—and even Germans—could have a grave where people could pray and place some flowers. But for my father it seemed this was not possible.

My mother had tried from the beginning to get

back her husband's poor remains; and even before she left Como she enlisted Gina's help. But to no avail. Then, in April 1946, when news came that the corpse had been stolen from the Musocco cemetery in Milan, she went to see Nenni, then Minister of the Interior. My mother recalls that Nenni, even though she and he had ceased to be friends many years before and had been divided by so much political hatred, was fairly courteous to her—as he was to my sister Edda, who went with my mother to see him about the matter on several subsequent occasions. But others came to power as the years went by and were not to prove so courteous. Not De Gaspari,* who several times turned down the plea of those two poor women, on the ground that "there were too many Fascists in Italy." Not even Pella,* though he was more polite and, through Andreotti,* gave back several letters my father wrote when he was a prisoner on the island of La Maddalena in August 1943. Not Scelba,* who was downright abusive and, even worse, encouraged my sister to hope that the body would be quickly handed over, so that my mother and Edda suffered even more cruelly. What made matters worse still was the behavior of members of the Government—indecisive, contradictory, unnecessarily mysterious, thus producing a continual stream of rumors according to which my father's remains were reported first here, then there. The reports were confirmed and denied, hopes rose

*All one-time Presidents of the Council of Ministers, and members of the Christian Democratic Party.

and were dashed, and the whole thing was at once macabre and ridiculous.

But let's say no more about it. On August 30, 1957, my mother won her last battle: she got back, for herself and for all of us, in circumstances which are too well known to need describing again, my father's body.

Now it lies in our home cemetery of San Cassiano at Predappio, next to my brother Bruno, Bruno's widow Gina, and our grandparents. Now that the storm seemed finally over, and eyes blinded by the red dust of war open again, my mother and her children could go every day and pray at those graves. I had already been back to visit the places where my father met his end. But it was a great day for me when at last I was able to visit my father's grave, not only because that grave and the peace in which my father can lie gave me strength, but also because none of this would have been possible if my mother and sister had not fought and suffered throughout all those years, for the sake of all of us, including me—and I was so far away. On that great day I thought of them with greater affection and deeper gratitude than ever before. Almost with affectionate envy—the envy one feels toward fellow beings who are out of the ordinary. They are the best of us, my mother and sister—which is why I have devoted most of this book to them.

But there are lots of us Mussolinis. Several are now dead, others have grown up and become men and women. We have all tried in one way or another to come with courage through the terrible ordeal of war, defeat, and persecution.

IX

We had all come back, arm in arm, from the midnight Mass. It was Christmas Eve, 1956, and to me Rome—the streets, the people, the festive mood—seemed more beautiful than ever before. It's Christmas and it's cold, I thought. It's cold here at Christmas time. When one is dazzled by too many vivid impressions, one always ends up by focusing on the least important things. Like the cold, for instance. For eleven years I had been living in Argentina, where Christmas comes in high summer, and wives and children go away on holiday and husbands stay and sweat in the city and receive from Europe those delightful cards with snow scenes that seem to depict another planet. Yet, before leaving for Argentina, I had lived thirty years in Italy. Time changes everything, ourselves included, even if we would have it otherwise. I looked around and couldn't believe it was all true. I was in Rome again, and with me were my mother, Romano, Anna Maria, and Edda.

And also Carolina Ciano, Marzio [Edda's son] and Marina [Bruno's daughter].

We were a family like any other, coming home from Mass and saying in chorus, "All the best. Happy Christmas!" to neighbors we met in the street. We all went up to Edda's place, at 9 Via Angelo Secchi. Edda had a big Christmas tree, hung with lights and glittering balls. Under it was a pile of parcels and packages, wrapped in colored paper and gold ribbon. The loveliest and most expensive, as usual, were those from Edda. Romano, the jazz lover, sat down at the piano and sketched out a tune. It was the sweet old music of *Stille Nacht*. "What," I said, "are you as old as all that?" He gave me a cross look and said, in that strange man's voice—strange to me because I had last seen him when he was still a boy—"No, I'm not old. But it's Christmas, so just listen, if you can. It's beautiful." He was right. Everything was wonderful that night.

The servant called us to supper. At the head of the table sat Carolina Ciano, still elegant, gay, and youthful. Edda and my mother sat on either side of her. It was the first time in thirteen years (apart from the brief gathering in Pompeii) that we had all been together, the first time since that day in Munich. So much had happened in the meantime. My father and Galeazzo were dead, and though none of us would say it, we were all aware of their absence. It was something we felt deep down, but without the agony any more. Time had softened our grief, had removed the scars of conflict and tragedy. The memory of our dead had created a more complete feeling of togetherness, an even closer link among those of us who lived on—and that was our happiness.

"And how's Dindina?" said my mother, switching the conversation to somebody who was absent because she hadn't been able to come to Rome. So we started talking about Dindina, Edda's daughter, who on that day in Munich had been barely nine years old. But now she was grown up and married, and lived with her husband in Brazil. Edda talked about her in her usual cheerful, ironical manner, under which she tried to hide that subtle emotion all mothers feel when they talk about a married daughter. I looked at her, and once again I could hardly believe that the crazy sister I could remember in short socks and with legs covered with scratches and bruises, already had a married daughter.

We all talked happily until four o'clock in the morning. We weren't aware of the time, as we recalled so many memories, some vivid, some vague, so many names and so many faces. It's always the women who are best informed about family affairs, and that night I realized I had a large number of relations, several of whom I had never known existed. My ignorance was partly due to something my mother has always firmly believed and practised: keeping relations at a distance, both her own and those of my father, so that nobody could accuse the Mussolinis of nepotism. "Napoleon," my mother used to say when my father wanted to allow some very small favor, "was ruined by his relations. I'm not letting it happen to you."

In this as in other things my mother was completely uncompromising—and my father didn't disagree with her. But he didn't want to go to the other extreme and hurt people to whom he was attached by family affection, just to avoid possible charges of nepotism.

And I am bound to say that events have proved my mother wrong. Our closest relations, those who in the days when our fortunes were riding high did not ask the smallest favor of my father, were the first to rally around when things went wrong; they showed a nobility of spirit all the more remarkable when one remembers they were ordinary farming or lower-middle-class people who for generations had usually been up against it, and had had to work hard for a meager living.

The first reliable records of the Mussolini family go back to the second half of the seventeenth century. Paolo Mussolini had a son, Francesco Mussolini, who married Benedetta Tartagni. That marriage produced in 1702 a second Paolo, who married Maria Francesca Ghetti. Her son, Giacomo Antonio, married first Maria Francesca Montaguti and, later, Maria Paganelli. By this second wife Giacomo had a son, Giuseppe Domenico Gaspare, in 1769. Giuseppe married Maria Angela Frassinetti, who bore him a son, Luigi, in 1805. Luigi married Maria Domenica Frignani, by whom, in 1834, he had a son who was called Luigi Agostino Gaspare. Luigi Agostino Gaspare died in 1908, but from his marriage with Caterina Vasumi four children were born, two boys and two girls—Alessandro, Alcide, Albina, and Francesca.

With Alessandro Mussolini, my father's father, a new trade came into our family, which up till then had always remained loyal to the land. The new trade was that of the blacksmith. Moreover, grandfather Alessandro was born at Collina (on November 11, 1854), while all his forebears had been born either at Calboli or Montemaggiore. How many Mussolinis have been born since then, and how many are alive today, it's not easy to say, and a clearer idea may emerge from the genealogical tree which I have tried to draw up. From time to time I receive letters written from the most unlikely places by people who bear my name or have some connection with it. My mother, especially, has a vast number of relations, as is common with the old farming families in Romagna. But what strikes me (indeed, to be honest, moves me) most, is that these people turn up, perhaps for the first time, when we have lost our special position and could do no more for them than could any other ordinary middle-class family, albeit a family with the great strength of being fondly united.

That is why I have for some years cherished the hope that one day we shall have a general reunion, as many old families do. I've already sent out a few letters, and the first replies have been very enthusiastic. But the problem, especially for those who live abroad, is to make the journey—it's a question of time and, even more, of money, because there isn't much of that in our family. As to the venue, I think there could be no place better than La Rocca delle Caminate.

La Rocca was till fairly recently still ours because the Italian Government let us keep it. The people of Romagna had donated it to us, each person subscribing a lira. It used to be so beautiful and majestic, with its ancient tower, its walls and big rooms and tricolor light. It suffered in the war: the tower was breached by Allied artillery, and Polish divisions camped in its rooms. The plunder was so complete, both then and later, that even the washbasins and pipes disappeared. The wooden floors were torn up, the doors and windows broken down—an example of senseless vandalism. To put La Rocca in order again would take many millions of lire, which none of us has. But I still think that for just one day, it could accommodate us somehow or other.

I remember when we used to gather up there every year for my father's birthday on July 29. In some things my father retained a simplicity that was almost childlike. The birthday party, the good wishes and little gifts from us all, spending a day far from his political commitments in the capital—he loved all this, and sometimes this man who never thought of himself would authorize some extra expenditure for his birthday celebrations.

It was nearly always a hundred lire, which he gave me personally a week before the party. With it, I would set off for Faenza to get a supply of fireworks. They were made by a man who had a workshop in the medieval walls, and who supplied us for this event in the knowledge that he was the best and luckiest fireworks maker in Romagna.

I would go back to La Rocca and put the rockets and Catherine wheels in a safe place; then, with my brothers and sisters, I would plan the show. I became very good at it and used to win praise from my father—but not from my mother because, like all housewives, she had an instinctive suspicion of anything explosive. Besides, she looked with a certain irony on the fact that my father, conqueror of an empire, got so much enjoyment out of fireworks.

It was true: my father was a simple man, like the rest of us. Fate decreed that for many years our family history should be dramatic, stormy, and full of matters of great moment. And I am bound to say that still today, if I am to judge by the sensitive thermometer of journalistic interest, millions of people, in Italy and throughout the world, continue to be interested in us. But in essence we've always been the same, and nothing has ever changed: not when political fortune made us powerful, not now when we have taken our ordinary place in the world again, often in other countries, seeking and finding in ourselves the strength to overcome bitterness and difficulty with dignity. We have done it without forgetting the past—because it would be impossible to forget more than twenty years in the life of a family and at the same time a nation—but also without recrimination, and without hating anybody, because we know that my father wouldn't have wanted that. Father was incapable of hatred, and even the anti-Fascists, who unloaded all possible blame on him, could never accuse him of being hard or cruel; and the Fascists, or at least the most fanatical of them, have always reproached him for the very fact that he forgave too easily and with too much generosity.

So I believe it will be a lovely, serene moment when we all meet at La Rocca (and the thought is so dear to me that I can't help talking about it as if it were an accomplished fact, whereas it may be years before it becomes a reality).

The hours will pass so quickly on that day. Those of us who were children in the old days will go out and find the roads and fields and memories of that distant happy time; our sons and daughters, the children of the present, many of whom we shall be seeing for the first time, will get to know one another, will grow fond of one another, just as we are. And as evening comes on, we shall all go down to Predappio, where my father rests in peace at last. We shall say a prayer at his grave, and at Bruno's, and at those of our grandparents and Gina. We shall leave some flowers. We won't say anything—it won't be necessary.

But my wish to bring together, one day, all the direct and indirect relations of the Mussolinis, at La Rocca delle Caminate, has still not been granted. I still live in Buenos Aires, but I have been back to my homeland several times. And recently I have been spending a considerable part of each year with my mother at the Villa Carpena, Forli. Italy is drawing me back into herself again, and I am thinking of returning home for good, one day soon. I feel drawn to Romagna: its countryside and coast have a place in my heart, they fill me with memories, beautiful and sad, but always of a life lived through events of extraordinary interest which are now assuming historical importance.

For financial reasons my mother was compelled to sell La Rocca delle Caminate. She had received from all over the world much higher offers than the very low price for which she decided to sell it to the Opera Nazionale Maternità ed Infanzia [National Nursery School organization], with an undertaking from the buyers that it would be made into a center for handicapped children. I must add that this undertaking has not been kept. La Rocca is even more dilapidated than before, and has now been given over to the Province of Forli—something we maintain to be illegal, and which is currently being taken before the courts. So, if I wanted to have a family reunion at La Rocca delle Caminate, it wouldn't be in my own home! However, during the last few years I have met, little by little, nearly all the Mussolinis and their collaterals still living. There are very many of us: my mother already has ten grandchildren and eleven great-grandchildren. Fortune has not always smiled, the family has had its ups and downs, and not all the marriages have been happy. But we are united, we are fond of one another, and we have none of us changed our ideas—except for a cousin of mine who is a Communist.

So if the family reunion has still not taken place, the bonds of affection have become stronger and have extended to our descendants. It is around my mother that the family really revolves. She is the family's supreme authority, and we are devoted to her. She is eighty-two years old, but still full of vitality— indeed it is renewed every day, as she takes a keen interest in all that goes on in the world, especially in Italy. The reunion could, in fact, be held here at the Villa Carpena, the old house in the outskirts of Forli, which was built in 1924 on the foundations of a farmhouse and has belonged to my mother for over fifty years (Romano and Anna Maria were born here). After all, this is our real home; everything here is the loving work of my mother—from the leafy trees to the vegetable garden, from the roses to the chicken run. And all the furniture and furnishings she has paid for twice over, because what wasn't confiscated was stolen.

But what really stopped me from arranging the reunion were the premature deaths of two of my cousins, of whom I was very fond—Vito Mussolini, son of Arnaldo, the Duce's brother, and Vanni Teodorani, whom I have already mentioned. There was also the incredible and very distressing death of my sister, Anna Maria. When at last life smiled on her from the eyes of two beautiful daughters, a cruel disease took her from them in 1968, when she was only forty.

Today the number of coffins lying in the family crypt in the cemetery of San Cassiano has been increased: as well as Anna Maria's, there is the one my mother has already had made, in hard granite quarried from around La Rocca. As always, my mother doesn't want to be taken by surprise or to rely on other people. Those who visit the crypt look at this half-open coffin and ask who lies inside. The attendant tells them of the farsighted action taken by Donna Rachele. But the death of Anna was a terrible blow to the whole family. Things took on a different aspect, some of our enthusiasm was dampened, and our gaiety became more restrained and silent.

Our family nurtures hate for nobody, and sincerely wishes for peace and harmony among Italians and a genuine coming together of the two factions into which defeat in war divided the Italian people. But the so-called victors, who ought to show the greater magnanimity, go on fanning the flames of hate. Proof of this was the criminal attempt made on Christmas night, 1971, when unknown hands placed a bomb at the door of the Mussolini Chapel at San Cassiano. The damage was extensive, but by good fortune the graves were left intact. It was a sad Christmas Day for all of us, but especially for my mother, who had been going every day to the cemetery to lay flowers on the graves of her dear ones, though there were flowers there already in abundance, brought by visitors from all over the world. Perhaps that was why the bomb was put there—to stop the tens and tens of thousands of people who come to Predappio to pay their respects to the Duce. Perhaps that is why the Social-Communist Council of Predappio still today procrastinates about giving us permission to carry out the necessary repairs and has ordained that the crypt should be kept closed. There are mean, small-minded men who don't realize that the judgment of history is sweeping away lies and falsehoods.

So we still fight on—with my mother in the vanguard, directing operations. In Italy, the birthplace of law, justice is slow to come, but come it does; and against overbearing insolence, against calumny and those who abuse their power, one has to stand up, physically or in the courts.

My father foresaw it all when he wrote in *Vita di Arnaldo (The Life of Arnaldo)* in 1931, "I have only one wish: to be buried beside my own, in the cemetery at San Cassiano. I would be very ingenuous if I thought I would be left in peace after my death. Around the graves of the leaders of those great transformations called revolutions there can be no peace. But it will be impossible to cancel out what has been done, and my spirit, freed from the material world, will live on after this little earthly life, in the immortal and universal life of God."

Around the grave at San Cassiano there is no peace, twenty-seven years after his death. But as long as my mother is able, she will take flowers to adorn the crypt and will greet the thousands of visitors who come from all over the world to that remote corner of Italy, away from the main roads, to stand and meditate before the grave of Benito Mussolini.